# ACE YOUR

## SPACE

### SCIENCE

### PROJECT

# ACE YOUR SCIENCE PROJECT

# ACE YOUR SPACE SCIENCE PROJECT

Robert Gardner and
Madeline Goodstein

## GREAT SCIENCE FAIR IDEAS

**Enslow Publishers, Inc.**
40 Industrial Road
Box 398
Berkeley Heights, NJ 07922
USA

http://www.enslow.com

**Library of Congress Cataloging-in-Publication Data**

Gardner, Robert, 1929–
    Ace your space science project : great science fair ideas / Robert Gardner
      and Madeline Goodstein.
      p. cm. — (Ace your science project)
    Includes bibliographical references and index.
    Summary: "Presents several science experiments and project ideas
      about space"—Provided by publisher.
    ISBN-13: 978-0-7660-3230-9
    ISBN-10: 0-7660-3230-2
    1. Space sciences—Experiments—Juvenile literature.  2. Science projects—
      Juvenile literature.  I. Goodstein, Madeline P.  II. Title.
    QB500.22.G369 2009
    520.78—dc22
                                 2008004688

Printed in the United States of America

10 9 8 7 6 5 4 3 2 1

**To Our Readers:** We have done our best to make sure all Internet Addresses in this book were active and appropriate when we went to press. However, the author and the publisher have no control over and assume no liability for the material available on those Internet sites or on other Web sites they may link to. Any comments or suggestions can be sent by e-mail to comments@enslow.com or to the address on the back cover.

♻ Enslow Publishers, Inc., is committed to printing our books on recycled paper. The paper in every book contains 10% to 30% post-consumer waste (PCW). The cover board on the outside of each book contains 100% PCW. Our goal is to do our part to help young people and the environment too!

The experiments in this book are a collection of the authors' best experiments, which were previously published by Enslow Publishers, Inc. in *Science Fair Success Using Newton's Laws of Motion*, *Science Project Ideas About Space Science*, *Science Project Ideas About the Moon*, *Science Project Ideas About the Sun*, and *Science Projects About Methods of Measuring*.

**Illustration Credits:** Jacob Katari, Figures 6, 14, 15, 16, 17, 18, 19, 20, 21, 22, 23, 24, 25, 26, 27, 28, 29, 30, 31; Gary Koellhoffer, Figures 1, 2, 4, 5, 7, 8, 9, 10, 11, 12, 13, 37; Stephen F. Delisle, Figures 3, 32, 33, 34, 35, 36.

**Photo Credits:** © bubaone/iStockphoto.com, trophy icons; © Chen Fu Soh/iStockphoto.com, backgrounds; NASA-GRC, p. 98; NASA-JPL, p. 50; NASA-KSC, p. 100; © Peter Chen/iStockphoto.com, p. 3 (boy); Shutterstock, pp. 3 (objects), 12, 32, 70.

**Cover Photos:** © Peter Chen/iStockphoto.com (boy); Shutterstock (objects).

# CONTENTS

## CHAPTER 1

## The Nearby Sky                                    13

## CHAPTER 2

## The Nearby Sky and Beyond                     33

## CHAPTER 3

## The Sun: Our Very Own Star                    51

## CHAPTER 4

## The Moon: Our Neighbor in the Sky          71

⊙ *Indicates experiments that offer ideas for science fair projects.*

⊙ *Indicates experiments that offer ideas for science fair projects.*

# INTRODUCTION

When you hear the word *science*, do you think of a person in a white lab coat surrounded by beakers of bubbling liquids, specialized lab equipment, and computers? What exactly is science? Maybe you think science is only a subject you learn in school. Science is much more than that.

Science is the study of the things that are all around you, every day. No matter where you are or what you are doing, scientific principles are at work. You don't need special materials or equipment or even a white lab coat to be a scientist. Materials commonly found in your home, at school, or at a local store will allow you to become a scientist and pursue an area of interest. By making careful observations and asking questions about how things work, you can begin to design experiments to investigate a variety of questions. You can do science. You probably already have but just didn't know it!

Perhaps you are reading this book because you are looking for an idea for a science fair project for school and you are interested in space. Maybe you want to learn about Earth or the Moon or the other planets in our solar system. Perhaps you are fascinated by the Sun and other stars or the sky beyond. This book will provide an opportunity for you to learn all about space. It will provide opportunities to build sundials, spectroscopes, and even rockets. It will explore topics such as latitude, seasonal changes, eclipses, distances between stars, and the diameters of planets. If you are particularly interested in rockets, satellites, how humans study space, or life in space, something is sure to catch your interest in the last chapter. You will discover scientific principles that will help you expand your understanding of the sky above you and beyond!

# THE SCIENTIFIC METHOD

All scientists look at the world and try to understand how things work. They make careful observations and conduct research about a question. Different areas of science use different approaches. Depending on the phenomenon being investigated, one method is likely to be more appropriate than another. Designing a new medication for heart disease, studying the spread of an invasive plant species such as purple loosestrife, and finding evidence about whether there was once water on Mars all require different methods.

Despite the differences, however, all scientists use a similar general approach to do experiments. It is called the scientific method. In most experiments, some or all of the following steps are used: making an observation, formulating a question, making a hypothesis (an answer to the question) and prediction (an if-then statement), designing and conducting an experiment, analyzing results and drawing conclusions, and accepting or rejecting the hypothesis. Scientists then share their findings with others by writing articles that are published in journals. After—and only after—a hypothesis has repeatedly been supported by experiments can it be considered a theory.

You might be wondering how to get an experiment started. When you observe something in the world, you may become curious and think of a question. Your question can be answered by a well-designed investigation. Your question may also arise from an earlier experiment or from background reading. Once you have a question, you should make a hypothesis. Your hypothesis is a possible answer to the question (what you think will happen). Once you have a hypothesis, it is time to design an experiment.

In many cases, it is appropriate to do a controlled experiment. This means there are two groups treated exactly the same except for the single factor that you are testing. That factor is often called a variable. For example, if you want to investigate the effect of surface area on a falling object, two groups may be used. One group is called the control group, and the other is called the experimental group. The two groups should be treated exactly the same except for the variable being tested. Suppose you conduct an experiment to investigate whether surface area of a ball affects how quickly it will drop. You might use balls of different sizes (and therefore surface area). The balls should be of equal weight and should be dropped from the same height. The variable is surface area; it is the only difference between the two groups.

During the experiment, you will collect data. In this case, you might use a stopwatch to time how long it takes for each ball to reach the ground. You might also calculate the surface area of each ball. By comparing the data collected from the control group with the data collected from the experimental group, you can draw conclusions. Since the two groups were exactly alike except for surface area, a shorter falling time would allow you to conclude with confidence that it is the result of the one thing that was different: surface area.

Two other terms that are often used in scientific experiments are *dependent* and *independent* variables. The dependent variable here is falling time, because it is the one you measure as an outcome and it depends on the ball's surface area. Surface area is the independent variable; it is the one that the experimenter intentionally changes. After the data is collected, it is analyzed to see if the hypothesis was supported or rejected. Often, the results of one experiment will lead you to a related question, or they may send you off in a different direction. Whatever the results, there is something to be learned from all scientific experiments.

## SCIENCE FAIR PROJECT IDEAS

Some of the experiments in this book may be appropriate for science fair projects. Experiments marked with a symbol (☻) include a section called Science Fair Project Ideas. The ideas in this section will provide suggestions to help you develop your own original science fair project. However, judges at such fairs do not reward projects or experiments that are simply copied from a book. For example, a model of the solar system, which is commonly found at these fairs, would probably not impress judges unless it was done in a novel or creative way. On the other hand, a carefully performed experiment to find out whether surface area affects how quickly an object falls would probably receive careful consideration.

## SCIENCE FAIRS

Science fair judges tend to reward creative thought and imagination. However, it's difficult to be creative or imaginative unless you are really interested in your project. Take the time to choose a topic that really appeals to you. Consider, too, your own ability and the cost of materials. Don't pursue a project that you can't afford.

If you decide to use a project found in this book for a science fair, you will need to find ways to modify or extend it. That should not be difficult because you will probably find that as you do these projects new ideas for experiments will come to mind. These new experiments could make excellent science fair projects, particularly because they spring from your own mind and are interesting to you.

If you decide to enter a science fair and have never done so before, you should read some of the books listed in the Further Reading section. The books that deal specifically with science fairs will provide plenty of helpful hints and lots of useful information that will enable you to avoid the pitfalls that sometimes plague first-time entrants. You will learn how to prepare appealing reports that include charts and graphs, how to set up and display your work, how to present your project, and how to relate to judges and visitors.

## SAFETY FIRST

As with many activities, safety is important in science and certain rules apply when conducting experiments. Some of the rules below may seem obvious to you, while others may not, but each is important to follow.

1. Have **an adult** help you whenever the book advises.

2. Never look directly at the Sun. It can cause permanent damage to your eyes!

3. All rocket experiments must be done with **adult supervision**. In all rocket tests, be sure that no person or object is close enough to be harmed by the launch or the rocket.

4. Wear eye protection and closed toe shoes (rather than sandals) and tie back long hair.

5. Don't eat or drink while doing experiments and never taste substances being used.

6. Do only those experiments that are described in the book or those that have been approved **by an adult**.

7. Never engage in horseplay or play practical jokes.

8. Before beginning, read through the entire experimental procedure to make sure you understand all instructions. Clear extra items from your work space.

9. At the end of every activity, clean all materials and put them away. Wash your hands thoroughly with soap and water.

## Chapter 1

# The Nearby Sky

IF YOU STEP OUTSIDE ON A CLEAR DAY AND LOOK UPWARD, YOU WILL SEE A BLUE DOME WE CALL THE SKY. Never look directly at the Sun. It can cause permanent damage to your eyes. The Sun, sometimes the Moon, and, if you look very carefully, the planet Venus can be seen on the surface of this dome, known to astronomers as the celestial hemisphere. At night you can see thousands of stars, sometimes the Moon, and often one or more planets. To most people, stars seem to be scattered across the sky in a random way, but others see definite patterns in the stars.

The Sun is the brightest star we see. With each rotation of Earth, the Sun rises and sets every day, giving us day and night. There are two explanations for the Sun's motion. One is that the Sun makes a circular path about Earth each day. The other is that Earth turns on its axis each day, which makes the Sun appear to move around Earth. You are probably convinced that the second explanation is the correct one, but do you have good experimental evidence to support your belief?

## WHERE ARE WE?

Positions on Earth are established from a giant imaginary grid that covers Earth's surface. These are the lines you see on maps or a globe. The lines that run north-south are called *meridians*. These lines measure *longitude*. The prime meridian is at zero (0°) longitude. It runs from the North Pole to the South Pole through Greenwich, England. If you look on a globe, you will see that the distance between longitude lines is greatest at the equator. The lines join to form a point at each pole.

The Sun seems to move in a circle around Earth once every 24 hours. Since there are 360 degrees (written as 360°) in a circle, the Sun moves 15° of longitude every hour. That is why time zones are about 15° apart. When you move westward from one time zone to the next, you set your clock back 1 hour. Why aren't all time zones exactly 15° apart?

Imaginary lines parallel to the equator are called *parallels*. They are used to measure *latitude*—degrees north or south of the equator. Degrees of latitude are about 111 km (69 mi) apart. The North Pole is 90° latitude. The equator is 0° (zero) latitude. This book was written at 42° latitude.

[ FIGURE 1 ]

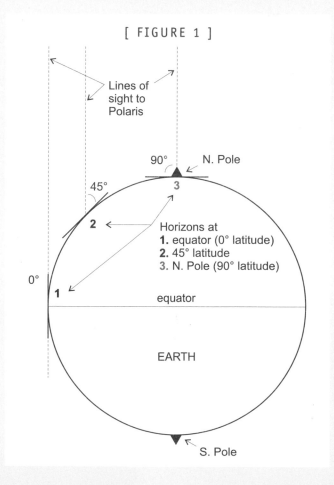

Lines of sight to Polaris

90°   N. Pole

45°

3

2

Horizons at
**1.** equator (0° latitude)
**2.** 45° latitude
**3.** N. Pole (90° latitude)

0°

1

equator

EARTH

S. Pole

# 1.1 Building an Astrolabe to Determine Latitude

Materials:

- straw
- square piece of cardboard
- protractor
- tape
- hole punch
- washer, nut, or sinker
- string
- paper clip
- a friend

Do you know the latitude where you live? You can make a pretty good estimate of your latitude by measuring the altitude of the North Star (Polaris), which is located almost directly above Earth's North Pole. As you can see from Figure 1, the altitude—the angle of elevation above the horizon—of Polaris is equal to the latitude from which its altitude is measured. Because Polaris is so far from Earth, light rays coming from the star are nearly parallel. Any that were not parallel would not strike Earth.

To find Polaris, go outside on a clear night. Look to the northern half of the sky to find the Big Dipper. It consists of a group of bright stars that look like the side of a cooking pan or water dipper as you see in Figure 2. Depending on the season and the time of night, the Big Dipper may be turned at different angles in the sky (see page 41 in Chapter 2). The pointer stars, Dubhe and Merak, form a line that points toward Polaris. The distance of Polaris from the Big Dipper is about five times the distance between these two pointer stars. Do not expect to find a very bright star. Polaris is about as bright as Merak. It is the star at the end of the handle of the Little Dipper.

To measure the altitude of Polaris, you can build an astrolabe like the one shown in Figure 3. When you look at the North Star through the soda straw, the string will hang along a line that measures the star's altitude. What is the altitude of Polaris? What is the latitude of your location?

[ FIGURE 2 ]

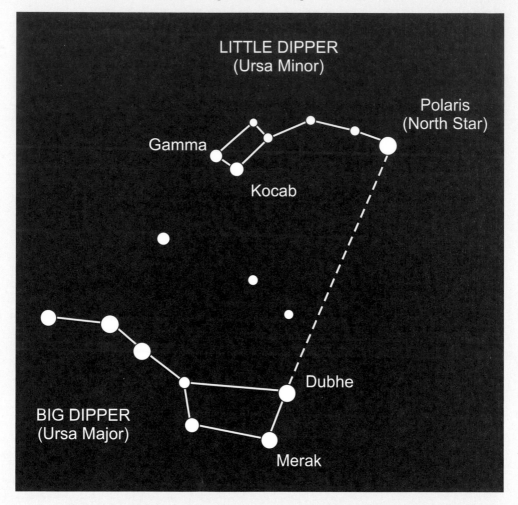

LITTLE DIPPER
(Ursa Minor)

Polaris
(North Star)

Gamma

Kocab

BIG DIPPER
(Ursa Major)

Dubhe

Merak

While you are measuring the North Star's altitude, have someone help you mark a north-south line of sight along level ground. While you stand looking at Polaris, you can direct your helper so that he or she is in line with Polaris. This will allow you to establish a straight line from the star to you. Markers at your position and the position of your helper will provide a north-south line that you will find useful in later experiments.

[ FIGURE 3 ]

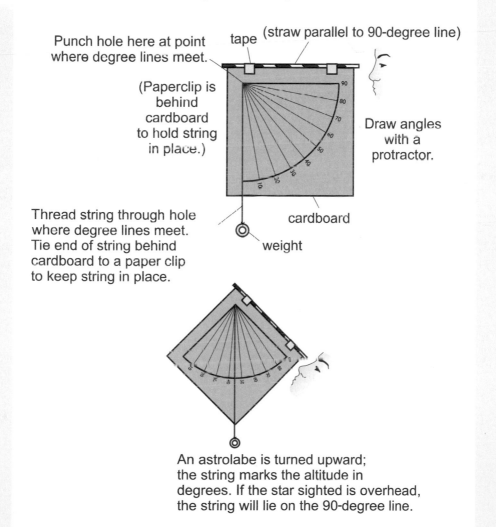

Punch hole here at point where degree lines meet.

tape (straw parallel to 90-degree line)

(Paperclip is behind cardboard to hold string in place.)

Draw angles with a protractor.

Thread string through hole where degree lines meet. Tie end of string behind cardboard to a paper clip to keep string in place.

cardboard

weight

An astrolabe is turned upward; the string marks the altitude in degrees. If the star sighted is overhead, the string will lie on the 90-degree line.

Materials:

- an adult
- hand drill
- square board, about 30 cm (12 in) on a side
- ruler
- new, unsharpened pencil
- pencil sharpener
- sandpaper
- carpenter's level
- white paper
- scissors
- tape
- protractor
- tape measure
- map pins and mesh strainer, or colored pens and clear dome

The Sun does not follow the same path across the sky each day. The summer Sun follows a longer and higher path than does the winter Sun. To find the path of the Sun at various times of the year, you can build a sundial.

**Ask an adult** to drill a hole in a 30-cm (12-in) square board; the hole should have the same diameter as a new, unsharpened pencil. The hole should be near the center of one side of the board and about 5 to 7 cm (2 to 3 in) in from the side as shown in Figure 4. Break off the eraser end of the pencil and sharpen it. Then, to prevent injury, break off the lead and sandpaper the end into a smoothly rounded surface. Insert the unsharpened end of the pencil into the hole in the board. The pencil should rise about 10 to 13 cm (4 to 5 in) above the surface of the board. Place the sundial on a level surface along a north-south line such as the one you established while measuring the altitude of Polaris. The vertical shaft, which casts a

# Path of the Sun

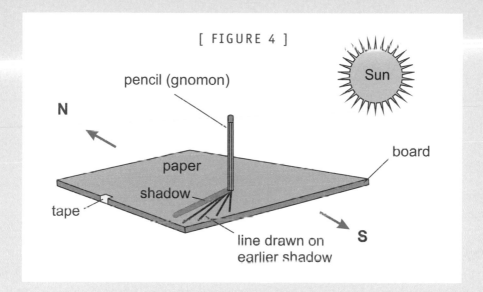

[ FIGURE 4 ]

pencil (gnomon)

Sun

N

board

paper

shadow

tape

line drawn on
earlier shadow

S

shadow, is called the *gnomon*. It should be near the south end of the board. Use a small carpenter's level to be certain the board is level and the pencil perpendicular to its surface.

Cover the board with a sheet of white paper. Cut a slit along the south edge of the paper so it will fit around the pencil and tape the paper to the board.

Early in the morning, when the Sun begins to cast shadows of the pencil on the paper, you can begin making measurements. With a ruler, draw a line along the center of the shadow from the pencil to the end of the shadow. (If the shadow should extend beyond the board, place another board beside your sundial and measure the total length of the shadow.) Measure the shadow from the center of the pencil to the end of the shadow. Write the length of the shadow and the time you made the measurement along the line you have drawn. Repeat this procedure at frequent intervals throughout the day.

To check the north-south line you made, take frequent measurements of the pencil's shadow around midday. The shortest shadow cast by the pencil will occur when the Sun is due south. At that time, the pencil's shadow will lie along a north-south line. Is the pencil's shortest shadow parallel to the north-south line you established earlier?

After sunset you can bring the paper inside and determine the Sun's position in the sky at various times during the day. Draw a north-south line (through the shortest shadow) and east-west lines on your paper. Each line should pass through the point where the pencil was located.

The Sun's azimuth is its angle along the horizon relative to north. North is 0°; east is 90°; south is 180°; and west is 270°. With a protractor, determine the Sun's azimuth for each line you drew.

The Sun's altitude is its angle above the horizon. If the Sun is on the horizon, its altitude is 0°. If it is directly overhead, its altitude is 90°. To determine the Sun's altitude at each of the times you measured it, draw a vertical line equal to the height of the pencil. At the base of this line, draw a line equal to the length of the pencil's longest shadow. (This line should make a right angle with the line representing the height of the pencil.) Mark the length of the shadow for each of the times you measured it on this line. A line connecting the shadow's length and the pencil's height will enable you to find the Sun's altitude for each of

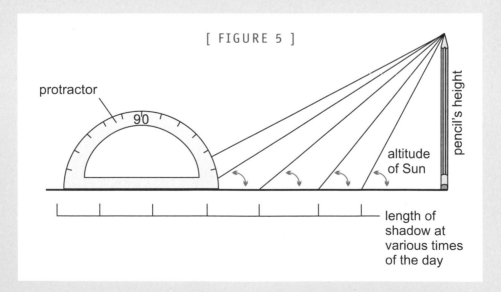

[ FIGURE 5 ]

protractor

90

altitude of Sun

pencil's height

length of shadow at various times of the day

the times you marked the Sun's shadow. Just lay a protractor on the angle as shown in Figure 5.

With the information you have, you can map with a sundial the Sun's position in the sky at each of the times you took a measurement (see Figure 6). You could use map pins in a wire mesh strainer or colored pen marks on a clear dome. Save this map of the Sun's path across the sky and compare it with other maps that you make at different times of the year. To see the biggest changes in the Sun's path, make measurements at the beginning of each season—around the twentieth of March, June, September, and December.

When is the Sun's path across the sky longest? When is it shortest? Does the Sun always rise at an azimuth of 90° and set at 270°? When does the Sun reach its greatest altitude?

[ FIGURE 6 ]

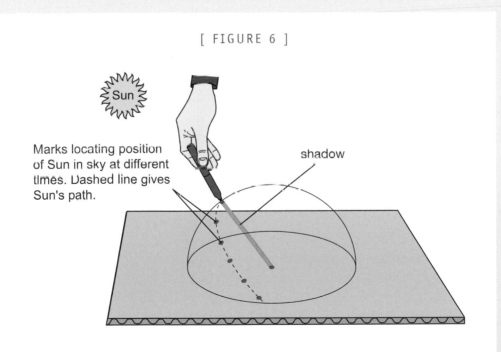

Sun

Marks locating position of Sun in sky at different times. Dashed line gives Sun's path.

shadow

# 1.3 What Causes Seasonal Changes?

Materials:
- light bulb
- table
- dark room
- small globe or ball
- tape
- cardboard tube
- flashlight
- white sheet of paper
- a partner
- pen or pencil

You know that the Sun's path across the sky changes from season to season. To explain seasonal changes on Earth, astronomers have found that Earth's axis is tilted at an angle of 23.5° relative to its orbit about the Sun. To see how this affects sunlight falling on Earth, place a bright light bulb in the center of a table in a dark room. Then move a small globe or a ball in a large circle around the bulb. Keep the ball or globe tipped at the same angle (see Figure 7) as you move it along its circular path. Stop at point S and turn the ball or globe to represent Earth's rotation on its axis. In which part of Earth does the Sun never set when it is at point S? In which part does the Sun never rise?

Repeat this process at point W. What seasons are represented by this model when Earth is at points S and W? How are the seasons different in the Northern and Southern Hemispheres?

To see how the angle at which light strikes Earth affects a season's average temperature, tape a long section of a cardboard mailing tube to the end of a flashlight. Place the end of the cardboard tube several inches above, and perpendicular to, a white sheet of paper as shown in Figure 8. Have a partner mark an outline of the light that falls on the paper. Keeping the tube the same distance from the paper, tilt the

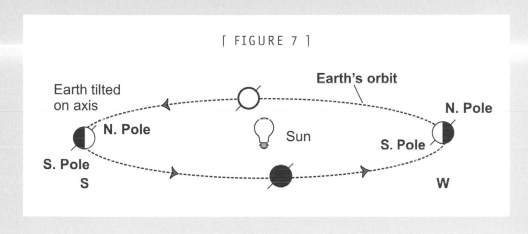

[ FIGURE 7 ]

Earth tilted
on axis

Earth's orbit

N. Pole

N. Pole

S. Pole

Sun

S. Pole
S

W

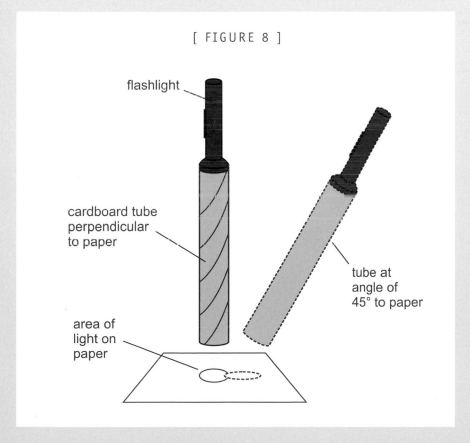

[ FIGURE 8 ]

flashlight

cardboard tube
perpendicular
to paper

tube at
angle of
45° to paper

area of
light on
paper

flashlight and tube so that the light falls on the paper at a different angle. Again, have someone mark the outline of the light on the paper. Continue changing the angle that the tube makes with the paper until the tube is almost parallel with the paper.

The amount of light coming through the tube is constant, just as light emitted by the Sun is constant. But what happens to the area of the light on the paper as the tube moves from a position perpendicular to the paper to one that is nearly parallel? Which condition is closest to summertime? to wintertime? How is the area over which the light energy spreads related to the season's average temperature?

# 1.4 Making a Model of the Moon's Path

**Materials:**

- globe
- can
- partner
- tennis ball
- long stick
- golf ball
- masking tape

Like the Sun, the Moon seems to circle Earth. But if you observe moonrise daily, you will see that it is about an hour later from one day to the next. You will notice, too, that the shape of the Moon changes dramatically over the course of a few days.

Try to observe the Moon over a period of several months. In your science notebook, make a daily sketch of its shape (when you can see it), a record of where it rises (azimuth) and/or sets, and its altitude and direction at different times. Do this as often as possible.

How does the position of a rising full moon compare with the position of the setting Sun on the same day? See if you can learn to predict the time, location, and shape of the rising Moon. How does the path of the Moon across the sky compare with the Sun's path?

You can make a model of the Moon's path about Earth that will help you understand why the Moon's shape changes. Place a globe, representing Earth, outside on a sunny day. Have a friend move a tennis ball about the globe, as shown in Figure 9, while you look at the ball with your eyes near the globe. Where, relative to Earth and the Sun, does the ball represent a full moon as seen from Earth? a first quarter? a last quarter? a new moon?

Using the model, when would you see a "full Earth" if you were on the Moon?

When Earth comes between the Moon and the Sun, Earth's shadow falls on the Moon, and we see an eclipse of the Moon. Where should the ball be placed to represent an eclipse of the Moon?

If the Moon comes between Earth and the Sun, it casts its shadow on Earth causing an eclipse of the Sun. Where should the ball be placed to represent an eclipse of the Sun? Do not look at the Sun!

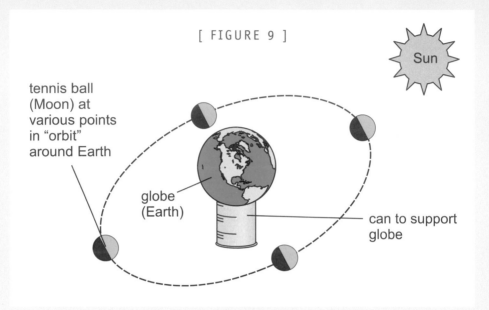

[ FIGURE 9 ]

Sun

tennis ball (Moon) at various points in "orbit" around Earth

globe (Earth)

can to support globe

Make a scale model of Earth and the Moon from the information in Table 1 about their diameters and separation. Use masking tape to attach the tennis ball labeled "Earth" to one end of a long stick that represents the distance from Earth to the Moon on your scale. Attach the golf ball labeled "Moon" to the other end. Take this model out into sunlight and move it about to produce eclipses. Why do eclipses occur so infrequently?

## TABLE 1

### Distance Between Earth and the Moon, and their Diameters

|  | Approximate distance |
| --- | --- |
| Earth to Moon | 384,000 km (240,000 mi) |
| Earth's diameter | 13,000 km (8,000 mi) |
| Moon's diameter | 3,500 km (2,150 mi) |

# Science Fair Project Idea

To see the Moon when it is a crescent, just after a new moon, you will have to view it shortly after sunset. You may be able to see a faint outline of the rest of the Moon as well as the bright crescent. This is sometimes called "the old moon with the new moon in its arms." The light beyond the crescent is due to earthshine, which is sunlight reflected from Earth to the Moon and then back to you.

If you have binoculars or a telescope, you will enjoy seeing a magnified image of the Moon and perhaps sense the same thrill that Galileo felt when he became the first human to view the lunar surface through a telescope. If you look along the terminator, the edge of darkness on the Moon, you will see that the long shadows cast there make the craters more distinct. Keep viewing the Moon from one new moon to the next. You will notice that you always see the same side of the Moon. What does this tell you about the Moon's period of rotation (time to turn once on its axis) as compared with its period of revolution (time to make one complete orbit around Earth)?

# 1.5 A Look at Some Planets

Except for the Moon, the brightest object in the night sky is Venus. It is often called the morning or evening "star." Of course, it is not a star. All the light we see from Venus, or any of the planets, is sunlight that is reflected from its surface. Because Venus is covered with clouds, about 80 percent of the sunlight that strikes the planet is reflected. (Only about 50 percent of the light striking Earth is reflected.) Since Venus's orbit is closer to the Sun than ours, Venus never appears very far from the Sun. Your newspaper will probably tell you the rising and setting times for Venus, so you should have no trouble finding it in the morning, before sunrise, or in the evening, after sunset, unless it happens to be very close to the Sun. Watch Venus for several months. What is the largest angle it makes with the Sun? You can use your fists to estimate this angle as the Sun sets or rises. **Remember: Never look directly at the Sun!**

If you locate Venus just before sunrise and keep track of its position, you will be able to see it even after the Sun rises. It is fun to point it out to others and show them that a "star" can be seen even in the daytime.

Again, with the newspaper to help you, you can probably locate the planet Jupiter, which is quite bright, and Mars, which is reddish. Mercury, which is never more than 28° from the Sun, and Saturn, the ringed planet, are more difficult to see, but with patience and persever-ance you can find them. Binoculars will help, but if you are looking for Mercury **do not look while the Sun is in the sky.** A number of moons orbit Jupiter, and you can see four of them with binoculars; however, you will probably have to mount the binoculars on a tripod or hold them against a firm object.

On a clear dark night you may see meteors, or shooting stars as they are often called. These are particles of matter that burn up when they hit Earth's atmosphere. There are particular places along Earth's orbit about the Sun where these particles seem to be concentrated. When Earth crosses these places, you can see 40 or 50 meteors per hour "shower" through the sky. The Perseid shower can best be seen about August 12 and the Geminid shower about December 13. The showers are named for the constellation where they appear in the sky. Most newspapers publish an article about these two meteor showers just before the showers occur.

## BODE'S LAW

During the late 1700s, astronomers developed a number scheme that became known as Bode's law. If you write down the series of numbers 0, 3, 6, 12, 24, 48, 96 . . . add 4 to each, and then divide each by 10, you obtain 0.4, 0.7, 1.0, 1.6, 2.8, 5.2, 10.0. . . .

You may think these are just a bunch of random numbers, but the numbers were significant to astronomers who often measure distances in astronomical units (AU). One astronomical unit is the distance from Earth to the Sun: 150,000,000 km (93,000,000 mi). If a planet were half as far from the Sun as Earth, the radius of its orbit would be 0.5 AU. A planet twice as far from the Sun as Earth would have an orbit with a radius of 2.0 AU.

Table 2 lists the planets and the radii of their orbits in astronomical units. Notice how closely the radii match the numbers in Bode's law. You can see why astronomers found Bode's law significant.

In 1781 the planet Uranus was discovered. It had a radius of 19.2 AU. This is close to the next number in the Bode's law series:

$$(192 + 4)/10 = 19.6.$$

## TABLE 2

### Some Planets and the Radii of Their Orbits in Astronomical Units (AU)

|  | Mercury | Venus | Earth | Mars | ? | Jupiter | Saturn |
|---|---|---|---|---|---|---|---|
| Radius (AU) | 0.38 | 0.72 | 1.0 | 1.52 | 2.8 | 5.2 | 9.54 |

The radii of the planets, including Uranus, are close to the numbers in the Bode's law series, but there is no planet at 2.8. During the nineteenth century, astronomers began to find small bodies at about 2.8 AU from the Sun, in the region between Mars and Jupiter. These bodies, with diameters of 1,000 km (600 mi) or less, are known as asteroids or minor planets. It used to be thought that the asteroids were the remnants of a planet that exploded. But it is more likely that they are particles from the original solar system that never came together to form a planet.

Meteoroids are believed to be material left by comets that broke up as they moved about the Sun. These particles continue to move along the comet's orbit—an orbit that crosses Earth's orbit. When they enter Earth's atmosphere, they are called meteors.

Occasionally a comet becomes visible as it moves close to the Sun. The orbits of comets are very long ellipses, unlike the nearly circular orbits of most planets.

A meteorite is a meteor that has survived its fiery path through the atmosphere and struck Earth. Some meteorites are huge. One that landed in Canada was nearly 3 km (2 mi) in diameter. An even larger one that struck Central America about 65 million years ago will be discussed in the next section. Fortunately, such large meteorites are very rare.

## LIFE ON EARTH

Though eight planets (Mercury, Venus, Earth, Mars, Jupiter, Saturn, Uranus, and Neptune) orbit the Sun, only Earth seems to harbor life. Mercury is sun-scorched. The surface of Venus, where it rains sulfuric acid, has a temperature of 480°C (870°F). The planets from Jupiter outward are very cold. Astronauts found our barren Moon, which has no atmosphere or water, to be lifeless. There is evidence of water on Mars, but landings there in 1976 by *Viking 1* and *Viking 2* revealed no evidence of life. Future trips to the red planet may provide different results. On Earth, the evolution of plants that can produce oxygen and food from water and carbon dioxide has provided an oxygen-rich atmosphere where animal life can prosper.

In 1953, Harold Urey and Stanley Miller mixed water vapor, methane, and ammonia in a flask. These gases are thought to have been present in Earth's early atmosphere. Electric sparks, similar to the lightning flashes that were probably prevalent in Earth's early days, were sent through these gases. At the conclusion of the experiment, the flask contained a variety of organic substances including amino acids, the building blocks of proteins. We still do not know how these substances gave rise to life, but we do know that the basic chemical ingredients of life could have been produced in Earth's primitive atmosphere.

We know also that about 65 million years ago 65 percent of the existing species on Earth became extinct. Recently, scientists have found a thin layer of iridium-rich dust in sites that are about 65 million years old. Since iridium is an element commonly found in asteroids and meteoroids, some scientists believe that a giant meteorite may have slammed into Earth at that time spewing huge clouds of dust into the atmosphere. The dust so reduced the sunlight reaching Earth that temperatures fell below levels necessary for the survival of many plants and animals. Following this long winter, the dust gradually settled, allowing sunlight to fall in abundance again on a planet now devoid of many of its previous life-forms.

## Chapter 2

# The Nearby Sky and Beyond

**THE EIGHT PLANETS AND THE ASTEROIDS THAT CIRCLE OUR SUN MAKE UP OUR SOLAR SYSTEM.** But what is the origin of the solar system and the stars that we see beyond it?

It is believed that gravity pulls together the star dust from earlier stars that blew apart to form new planets and stars. Gravity is the force of attraction that one piece of matter exerts on another. This force depends on the amount of matter, commonly called *mass*, in each piece and the distance between the masses. If the mass of either piece is doubled, the pull between them (force of attraction) doubles. If the distance between the pieces doubles, the force is reduced to one fourth of its former value.

Earth pulls on you. The force it exerts on you is called your weight. If a larger person has twice your mass, the gravitational force between that person and Earth is twice as great as the force between you and Earth. He or she weighs twice as much as you do. But if you doubled your distance from the center of Earth, Earth's pull on you at this greater distance would be much less. Your weight would be quartered.

Originally, the rotating star dust that formed our solar system was very cold. The only gases that could exist at such low temperatures were hydrogen and helium. All other matter was probably in the form of solid, dustlike particles. Gravitational pulls among the particles caused a general drift toward the center of the "cloud," producing a contraction of the matter and higher temperatures. Because of rotation, the cloud became a flattened disk. Near the center, where temperatures were higher due to greater pressure, a protosun formed. (*Proto-* means the earliest form of something.) Rotation kept some of the matter far from the center—out where it was still very cold.

Continued contraction of the central part of the disk raised temperatures to millions of degrees. At such a high temperature, hydrogen began fusing to form helium, like a giant hydrogen bomb. The energy released by fusion kept that reaction going while creating an outward pressure that balanced the inward gravitational contraction. Thus a stable star, our Sun, was born.

The small, dense, inner planets, Mercury, Venus, Earth, and Mars, formed during a period of 100 million years as particles of matter circling the Sun were pulled together by gravitational forces. These particles were rich in sulfur, silicon, iron, magnesium, and other metals from dead stars. The decay of radioactive elements, the violent impact of the colliding particles growing into planets, as well as heat from the growing star (Sun) nearby kept these materials in a melted state. The denser iron sank beneath the lighter matter. This explains why Earth has an iron core surrounded by less dense rock and silicon-rich sand. The high temperature caused molecules of hydrogen and helium to move so fast that they escaped from the atmospheres of these inner planets.

Each planet has an escape velocity. Anything moving faster than the escape velocity can escape the planet's gravity. On Earth, the escape velocity is about 40,000 km/hr (25,000 mph). Space probes sent from Earth to explore other planets had to be accelerated to the escape velocity in order to leave Earth and not be pulled back by gravity. The velocities of hydrogen and helium molecules, at the temperatures found on the inner planets, were large enough to escape the relatively weak gravity of these small planets.

The outer planets, Jupiter, Saturn, Uranus, and Neptune, are large and have low densities because so much of their matter is gaseous. They coalesced from particles of solid matter to form protoplanets. Temperatures so far from the Sun were low enough that the huge amounts of hydrogen and helium swept up by these planets as they moved along their orbits could not escape. As a result, the outer planets have Earth-sized cores of solid matter surrounded by thick gaseous atmospheres.

At about the time the planets reached their present size, the onset of fusion reactions at the Sun's core caused it to expel its outer matter. The solar system was essentially finished after the Sun began fusing hydrogen into helium.

Table 3 contains information about each of the planets in our solar system.

## TABLE 3

### Orbit and Composition Data for the Eight Planets

| Planet | Radius of orbit (AU) | Time to orbit Sun (in Earth years) | Diameter (Earth = 1) | Mass (Earth = 1) | Density (g/cm³) |
|---|---|---|---|---|---|
| Mercury | 0.39 | 0.24 | 0.38 | 0.06 | 5.4 |
| Venus | 0.72 | 0.62 | 0.95 | 0.82 | 5.2 |
| Earth | 1.0 | 1.0 | 1.0 | 1.0 | 5.5 |
| Mars | 1.52 | 1.88 | 0.53 | 0.11 | 3.9 |
| Jupiter | 5.2 | 11.86 | 11.3 | 318.0 | 1.3 |
| Saturn | 9.5 | 29.64 | 9.44 | 95.2 | 0.7 |
| Uranus | 19.2 | 84.01 | 4.10 | 14.5 | 1.2 |
| Neptune | 30.1 | 164.8 | 3.88 | 17.2 | 1.7 |

Materials:
- Table 3
- modeling clay
- soda straws
- ruler
- tape measure
- binoculars or telescope

The diameter of the Sun is about 1,400,000 km (868,000 mi), the distance from Earth to the Sun (the radius of Earth's orbit) is about 150,000,000 km (93,000,000 mi), and the diameter of Earth is about 13,000 km (8,000 mi). Using this information and the data in Table 3, use balls of modeling clay and soda straws to construct a model of the solar system. Your model will give you a good sense of the distances between planets, but it is almost impossible to make it to scale. Once you start building your model, you'll see why.

## THE MILKY WAY

Stars are not spread evenly through space. They cluster in groups called galaxies. Our own Sun is but one of the billions of stars that make up our galaxy. On a clear, moonless night, away from city lights, you can see a hazy band that stretches across the sky. Look at this band with binoculars or a telescope. You will see that it is made up of a vast number of stars. These stars make up our galaxy. (A galaxy is a large group of stars held together by gravity.) When we look at them, we are looking edge-on into the Milky Way galaxy, the galaxy in which our own Sun lies.

The Milky Way galaxy is about 100,000 light-years (ly) in diameter. A light-year is the distance that light travels in one year. Since the speed of light is 300,000 km/s (186,000 mi/s), and since there are about 31 million seconds in a year, a light-year is a distance of about 6 trillion miles. So, our galaxy is 600,000 trillion miles across. Such distances are hard to imagine, especially when you realize that our solar system is *only* about 10 billion miles in diameter. This means that 60 million solar systems like ours could fit into our galaxy. When you realize that there are galaxies out to at least 12 billion light-years from us, you begin to appreciate the vastness of the universe we live in.

If an inch were used to represent the diameter of Earth, the solar system, on this scale, would stretch halfway to the Moon. The Milky Way galaxy would extend beyond the Sun to Saturn.

Galaxies are usually far apart, but telescopes reveal that they sometimes merge or collide. Since galaxies are only about 100 diameters (10 million ly) apart and stars within galaxies are about 100 million diameters apart, it is not surprising that galaxies collide more often than stars.

## CONSTELLATIONS

The distance to the nearest star outside our solar system is about 4 light-years, but a near star may not appear as bright as a star that is much farther away. Stars that make up a constellation, such as the Big Dipper, may differ greatly in their distances from us. Between these bright stars are stars too dim to be seen with the naked eye. The stars that form a constellation are not necessarily very close together. And, because the stars in the constellations may be moving in different directions at different speeds, the constellations that we recognize today may look very different a few thousand years from now.

Because Earth moves about the Sun, the stars that we see when darkness falls change from month to month. The sky appears to turn about 30° from one month to the next because Earth moves about 30° along its 360° orbit in each of the 12 months. Ursa Major's position at 9 P.M. on October 1 will be the same as its position at 7 P.M. on November 1 or 11 P.M. on September 1. If you view the stars at the same time each night, they will appear to move about 2 hours (30°) westward from one month to the next.

Materials:

- a square of 0.2-cm-
  (1/16-in-) thick clear
  plastic, about 30 cm
  (12 in) on each side

- ruler
- scriber compass
- protractor
- marking pen
- plastic wrap
- heavy cardboard
- tape
- felt pen
- star chart
- flashlight
- red cellophane

Because the sky seems to rotate about Earth at a steady rate, you can build a sky clock that will allow you to tell time on clear nights. To make your sky clock you will need a square sheet of 0.2-cm- (1/16-in-) thick clear plastic. The piece should measure 30 cm (12 in) on each side. You can buy the plastic in an art store. Draw two straight lines forming right angles through the center of the sheet as shown in Figure 10. Place one point of a scriber attached to a compass at the center of the sheet. Use the other point of the scriber to scratch a circle with a radius of 5 1/4 in on the plastic sheet. Then draw additional circles with radii of 4 3/4, 4 1/4, and 3 in.

Use a protractor to break the circles into twelve 30-degree segments. With a marking pen, write the numbers found on a clock's face on your sky clock. Now divide each 30 degree segment in half. Use the marking pen to write in the months of the year and the 24 hours represented by the 15-degree lines. The numbers representing hours on the 24-hour inner circle are numbered in counterclockwise fashion because Earth turns counterclockwise as viewed from Polaris. Color the lines scratched in the plastic.

[ FIGURE 10 ]

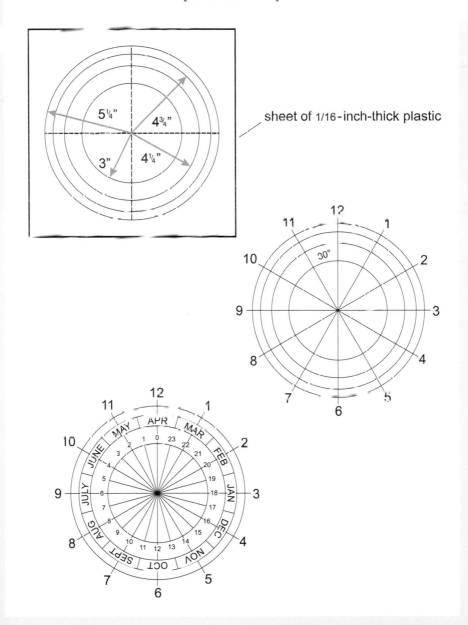

sheet of 1/16-inch-thick plastic

Another, less expensive way to make a sky clock is to stretch a sheet of plastic wrap over a 30 cm (12 in) square cut out of a larger sheet of heavy cardboard. Tape the plastic wrap firmly to the cardboard and draw the lines on the clear wrap with a felt pen.

Take your sky clock outside in the evening and early morning. Practice using it to tell time. Hold it so that its plane is perpendicular to, and its center in line with, Polaris. The numeral 12 directly above April should be at the top of the clock as would be the numeral 12 on a clock in your house. Read the position of the pointer stars of the Big Dipper on your sky clock. Together they form a line representing the hour hand of a clock.

The drawings in Figure 11 show the 9 P.M. positions of the pointer stars at mid-month for each month of the year. Using those drawings and the position of the pointer stars on your sky clock, you can make a good estimate of the time. For example, suppose it is mid-July. When you hold your sky clock properly, you see the pointer stars of the Big Dipper on your sky clock at the 6 o'clock position, as shown in Figure 12. The inner-numbered circle, which measures the 24 hours required for Earth to turn once on its axis, shows you that 6 hours (6 to 12) have passed since the pointer stars were at the 9 P.M. position, which is where they would be at 9 P.M. on July 15. Therefore, the time is 3 A.M.

Now, suppose it is November 23 and you see the pointer stars in the same 6 o'clock position. On November 15 at 9 P.M., you would expect the pointer stars to be in the 5 o'clock position. However, the inner circle shows you that these pointer stars are at a point 2 hours earlier than the 5 o'clock position (14 back to 12). If it were November 15, the time would be 7 P.M. Because it's about a week later than November 15, the clock position of the pointer stars at 9 P.M. will be at about 4:45. Consequently, the time is probably closer to 6:30 P.M.

## POLAR CONSTELLATIONS

Some bright constellations turn about Polaris. A star chart shows you those constellations. The brighter the star, the bigger the dot on the chart.

# [ FIGURE 11 ]

### JANUARY
(3 o'clock at 9 P.M.)

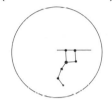

### FEBRUARY
(2 o'clock at 9 P.M.)

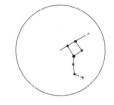

### MARCH
(1 o'clock at 9 P.M.)

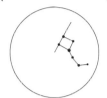

### APRIL
(12 o'clock at 9 P.M.)

### MAY
(11 o'clock at 9 P.M.)

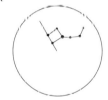

### JUNE
(10 o'clock at 9 P.M.)

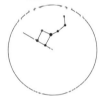

### JULY
(9 o'clock at 9 P.M.)

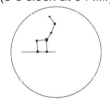

### AUGUST
(8 o'clock at 9 P.M.)

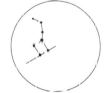

### SEPTEMBER
(7 o'clock at 9 P.M.)

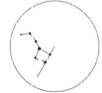

### OCTOBER
(6 o'clock at 9 P.M.)

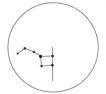

### NOVEMBER
(5 o'clock at 9 P.M.)

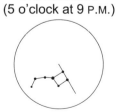

### DECEMBER
(4 o'clock at 9 P.M.)

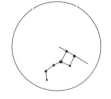

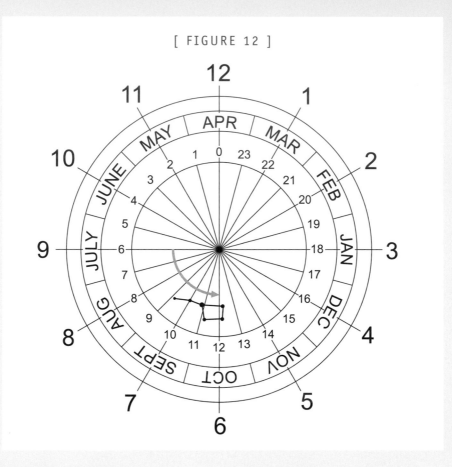

[ FIGURE 12 ]

Take a star chart outside. Tape red cellophane over the glass of a flashlight. In that way, you will not lose your night vision when you shine the light on the chart. Place the appropriate month of the year uppermost against the northern sky to find the constellations. Can you find all the constellations on the chart?

## TYPES OF STARS

Stars are classified according to their surface temperature. Astronomers can determine a star's temperature by the type of light it emits. Red stars are cooler than blue stars as you can see from Table 4.

## TABLE 4

### Star Types and Their Characteristic Temperatures and Colors

| Star Type | Temperature (°C) | Color | Example |
|---|---|---|---|
| O | >35,000 | Green- or blue-white | Rare |
| B | 10,000–35,000 | Hot white | Rigel in Orion |
| A | About 10,000 | Cool white | Sirius in Canis Major |
| F | 6,000–10,000 | Slightly yellow | Polaris |
| G | About 6,000 | Yellow | The Sun |
| K | About 4,000 | Orange | Arcturus in Boötes |
| M | About 3,000 | Red | Betelgeuse in Orion |

## Science Fair Project Idea

With a little practice, you will be able to estimate time quite accurately with your sky clock. If you live near the eastern or western end of a time zone, your clock will appear to be a little fast or slow. How can you adjust your time estimate? Since the sky clock is set for standard time, how can you adjust your estimate for daylight saving time?

# 2.3 Building and Using a Spectroscope

**Materials:**

- scissors
- shoe box
- cardboard
- tape
- diffraction grating
- black construction paper
- showcase lamp or unfrosted light bulb
- fluorescent light bulb
- neon light
- large cardboard box
- white paper
- a friend

To examine the light emitted by stars, astronomers use spectroscopes. A spectroscope is a device that separates light into the various colors that make it up. Light has wavelike properties, and we find that red light has a longer wavelength than blue light. To separate ordinary white light into its various colors or wavelengths, you can build a simple spectroscope.

Cut two small square holes in opposite ends of a shoe box. Cover one of the holes with two small pieces of cardboard so that they form a narrow slit as shown in Figure 13. Tape a piece of diffraction grating over the other hole. But before you fix it in place, hold it up toward a light. Turn it so that, when light comes through the grating, the light spreads out into a *horizontal* spectrum of colors. You can buy diffraction gratings in a hobby shop or order one from a scientific supply company. Cover the rest of the inside of the box with black construction paper and tape it shut.

Hold the spectroscope so that the slit in the box is parallel with the bright filament of a showcase lamp or an unfrosted light bulb. Look to either side of the slit. You will see a spectrum containing all the colors of the rainbow. Look at a fluorescent light bulb. You will see not only a

[ FIGURE 13 ]

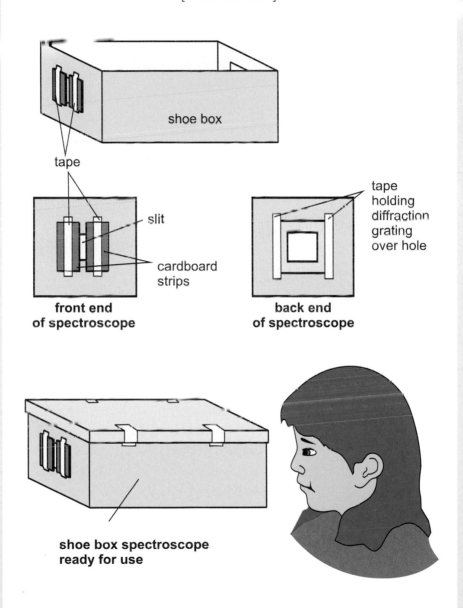

tape

front end
of spectroscope

slit

cardboard
strips

tape
holding
diffraction
grating
over hole

back end
of spectroscope

shoe box spectroscope
ready for use

shoe box

spectrum, but also the bright violet, green, and yellow lines emitted by the mercury vapor inside the bulb. Like mercury, each element emits characteristic wavelengths or colors. Look at a neon light. What colors are released by neon? With spectroscopes, astronomers can figure out what elements are in stars.

To see the colors in sunlight, cut a small hole in one side of a large cardboard box. The hole should be in the middle of the side near the bottom. Tape a piece of diffraction grating over the hole. Then tape a sheet of white paper to the inside of the box on the side opposite the hole. Turn the box upside down and get inside with your back toward the diffraction grating. **Remember: Never look at the Sun.** Have a partner help you turn the box so that sunlight falls onto the grating. Look on the white screen to see the colors found in sunlight. To view a solar eclipse, substitute a pinhole for the diffraction grating. Don't look at the pinhole. Look at the whole screen.

When a star is coming toward us at high speed, the wavelengths of the light it emits are shorter than normal. If the star is traveling away from us, its light waves are "stretched" into longer wavelengths. This phenomenon is known as the Doppler effect. You have probably observed this effect with sound. If a car is approaching you with its horn blaring, the pitch seems higher than normal because the vibrations are more frequent than normal. The sound waves are "squeezed" together because the horn is traveling toward you as it emits sound waves. Thus, one wave follows the next sooner than it would if the car were at rest. When the car passes you and moves away, the pitch seems lower than normal. The car is moving away from the waves that strike your ear, so the waves are "stretched" and reach you less frequently than they normally would.

In the case of receding stars, astronomers say the light has a red shift because the wavelengths of the light emitted are longer than would be the case if the star were at rest. Similarly, approaching stars show a blue shift. Knowing the speed of light and the amount that known wavelengths emitted by various elements in the stars are shifted, astronomers can determine the speed that stars are moving toward or away from us. By comparing the red shifts or blue shifts of stars turning on their axes, astronomers can tell which way a star is spinning. Further, from the red shifts seen in galaxies, there is good evidence that the universe is expanding and that the farther a galaxy is from us, the faster it is moving away.

# 2.4 What Is Parallax?

Materials:

-library

-computer access to the Internet (optional)

-index cards

-pen

-calculator (optional)

In astronomy books, you might find a table like Table 5, which lists a number of stars and their distances from Earth. Notice that the distances to these stars are measured in light-years. A light-year is the distance light travels in one year. This means that the light we see when we look at the star Spica left that star 260 years ago, during Colonial times in America.

## TABLE 5

### Some Well-Known Stars with Their Distances from Earth as Measured in Light-Years

| Star's Name | Distance from Earth in light-years |
|---|---|
| Alpha Centauri | 4.2 |
| Barnard's star | 6.0 |
| Sirius | 8.8 |
| Altair | 17 |
| Vega | 26 |
| Arcturus | 36 |
| Castor | 45 |
| Capella | 46 |
| Aldebaran | 68 |
| Spica | 260 |

Do some research to find out how astronomers use parallax to measure the distance to nearby stars. Then try to find out how they measure the distance to stars and galaxies that are thousands, millions, and billions of light years from us.

In Experiment 2.1, you calculated the distance, in kilometers, equal to a light-year. What is the length of a light-year in miles? Sirius is the brightest star in the sky. In kilometers, how far from Earth is Sirius? If you were in a spaceship traveling at an average speed of 300 km/s, how long would it take you to reach Alpha Centauri, the closest star to Earth (other than our Sun)?

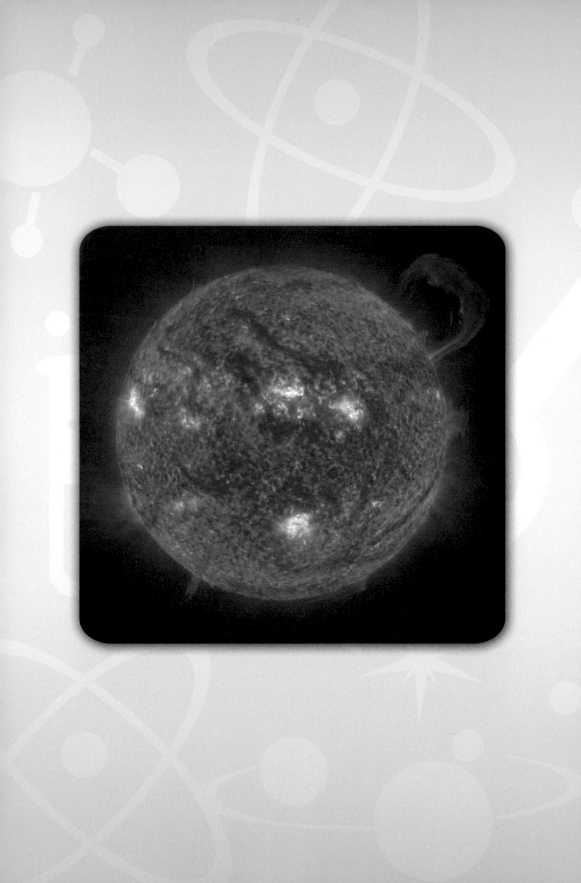

## Chapter 3

# The Sun: Our Very Own Star

**DID YOU KNOW THAT WE HAVE OUR VERY OWN STAR? THAT STAR IS THE SUN.** Because the Sun appears to be so much bigger than all the other stars we see, we normally don't think of it as a star. But it is! It looks much bigger than other stars because it is so close to us. You know from Chapter 2 that it is only 150 million kilometers (93 million miles) from Earth.

You may not think of the Sun as being close to Earth. To travel that far, you would have to circle Earth 3,750 times. Even the light from the Sun takes 8 minutes and 20 seconds to reach Earth. But compared to other stars, the Sun is not far away at all. To get to the next closest star, you would have to travel 40 trillion kilometers (40,000,000,000,000 km), or 25 trillion miles. Even if you could travel at the speed of light, it would take you more than four years to reach that star.

The Sun is much bigger than Earth. Recall that Earth's diameter (the distance from one side to the other through the center) is approximately 13,000 km (8,000 mi). The Sun's diameter is 1.4 million kilometers (868,000 mi). So the Sun's diameter and circumference (girth or distance around) are 109 times bigger than Earth's. But its volume is 1,300,000 times greater than Earth's. Do you see why? (If you don't, you will after you do Experiment 3.1.)

The Sun is much hotter than Earth. While the average temperature on Earth's surface is 20°C (68°F), the Sun's surface temperature is 5,500°C (9,900°F). At the Sun's center, the temperature is about 16,000,000°C (29,000,000°F). However, at Earth's core, the temperature is only 6,500°C (12,000°F).

The Sun is 330,000 times more massive than Earth. The Sun's mass is nearly 2 million trillion trillion kilograms (a 2 followed by 30 zeros) or 2 thousand trillion trillion tons. Earth is only 6 trillion trillion kilograms (a 6 followed by 24 zeros). It is the Sun's huge mass that gives it the gravitational force needed to make all the planets revolve around it.

The matter that makes up the Sun is mostly hydrogen (75 percent) and helium (24 percent). The remaining 1 percent is made up of the other elements. Nuclear reactions go on within the Sun. These reactions produce the vast energy the Sun emits each second. The 400 trillion trillion watts of power the Sun releases provides its luminosity, which is a measure of its brightness. The Sun produces a lot of energy, but many stars produce more and are much more luminous. Sirius, the brightest star in our sky, is 23 times brighter than our Sun. Other stars are thousands of times brighter than the Sun, but some of them are so far away that they cannot be seen without a telescope.

Earth's orbit about the Sun is not a perfect circle. It is slightly elliptical (oval). The elliptical nature of Earth's orbit is exaggerated in Figure 14. This is done to show that the distance between Earth and the Sun does change. Earth is at perihelion (closest to the Sun) in early January when it is about 147 million kilometers (92 million miles) from the Sun. It is at aphelion (farthest from the Sun) in early July when the Sun is about 152 million kilometers (95 million miles) from Earth. As you can see, our distance from the Sun does not change very much. But you may wonder how the Northern Hemisphere can have winter when Earth is closest to the Sun and summer when Earth is farthest from the Sun. Go back to Experiment 1.3 to figure out the reason.

Earth's average speed along its orbit about the Sun is 29.8 km/sec or 18.6 mi/sec. Its speed is slightly greater when it is closer to the Sun and slightly less when it is farther from the Sun. Therefore, Earth moves slightly faster around the Sun in the winter and a bit more slowly in the summer.

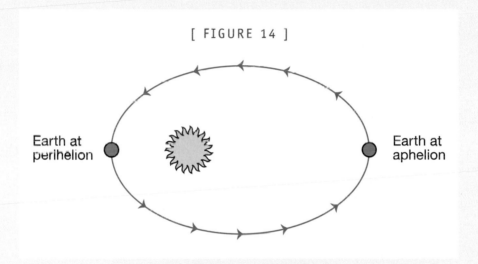

[ FIGURE 14 ]

Earth at
perihelion

Earth at
aphelion

Earth's elliptical orbit about the Sun is shown. The elliptical nature
of the orbit is greatly exaggerated; it is really almost a circle.

Materials:
-clay
-ruler

You know that the Sun's diameter and girth are 109 times bigger than Earth's. Yet, its volume is more than a million times greater. To see why this is true, begin by making a cube from clay. A cube is a block that has the same length, width, and height. Using the clay and ruler, make a cube that is 1 cm on each side, as shown in Figure 15. How many faces does the cube have?

The area of the surface of each face is found by multiplying the length of the face by its width (its length times its width). If the length and width are measured in centimeters, the area will be in square centimeters (sq cm). As you can see, the surface area of one face of the cube you have made is:

$$1 \text{ cm} \times 1 \text{ cm} = 1 \text{ sq cm, or } 1 \text{ cm}^2$$

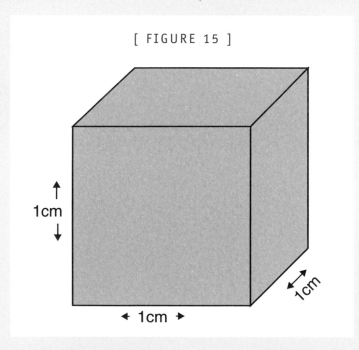

[ FIGURE 15 ]

1cm

1cm

1cm

A cube of clay 1 centimeter (cm) on a side is shown.

What is the total area of all the cube's six faces?

The volume of the cube you have made is the space that it occupies. Space has three dimensions: length, width, and height. The volume of any cube can be found by multiplying its length by its width by its height (volume = length × width × height). The volume of your cube will be in cubic centimeters (cu cm). The cube you have made is 1 cm long, 1 cm wide, and 1 cm high. Therefore, the volume of the cube you made is:

$$1 \text{ cm} \times 1 \text{ cm} \times 1 \text{ cm} = 1 \text{ cu cm, or } 1 \text{ cm}^3$$

Now make a second cube of clay. Make this one 2 cm wide, 2 cm long, and 2 cm high. Place the second cube beside the first. (1) How many of the small cubes would you need to put together to have a face with the same area as one face of the larger cube? (2) What is the area, in square centimeters, of each face of the larger cube? (3) What is the total area of all the cube's six faces? (4) How does the total area of this cube compare with the total area of the first cube?

Again, place the first cube beside the second one. (5) How many times would the small cube fit into the larger cube?

Multiply the length of the larger cube by its width and height. (6) How many cubic centimeters are occupied by the larger cube? (7) How does the volume you found in question 6 compare with the volume of the larger cube that you found in question 5? You can check your answers to questions 1 through 7 by turning to page 122.

Now let's return to the question about the Sun's diameter and volume as compared with Earth's. Think of Earth as a cube. Think of the Sun as a cube that is 100 times as wide. As you can see from Figure 16, you could place 100 Earths along each edge of the Sun. Then you would have to stack 100 rows of 100 Earths before you covered one face of the Sun. Finally, you would have to make 100 more such stacks before you had a cube as thick as the Sun. All together, you would have to use 100 × 100 × 100 Earth cubes to make a cube the size of the Sun. How many Earth cubes will fit into the Sun cube?

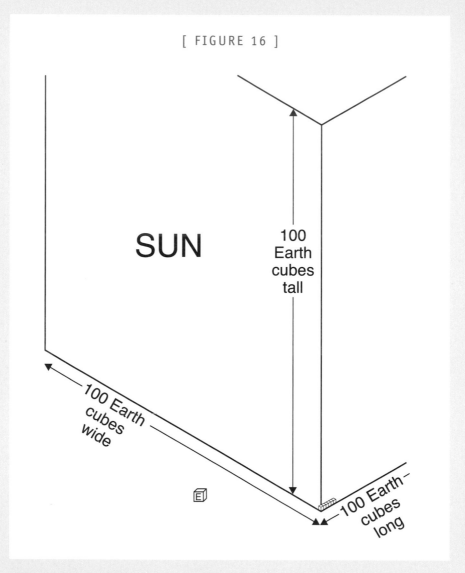

[ FIGURE 16 ]

SUN

100
Earth
cubes
tall

100 Earth
cubes
wide

100 Earth
cubes
long

**Earth and Sun are shown as cubes. The Sun is approximately 100 times longer, wider, and taller than Earth.**

The Sun is actually 109 times the diameter of Earth. If you multiply 109 × 109 × 109, your answer will be just about 1,300,000 (1.3 million). That is why the Sun's volume is 1,300,000 times greater than Earth's, even though its diameter is only 109 times bigger than Earth's.

## ECLIPSES OF THE SUN AND MOON

Just as you cast a shadow on Earth, so may the Moon. The Moon's shadow is seen when the Moon comes between the Sun and Earth (see Figure 17a) during a new moon. It is called an eclipse of the Sun (a solar eclipse) because the Sun, or part of it, is hidden by the Moon. Since the Moon is much smaller than the Sun, its shadow covers only a small part of Earth. And the Moon's shadow, like yours, has a dark portion (umbra) and a fuzzy portion (penumbra). The umbra touches only a tiny part of Earth's surface, if any. Therefore, only a small area of Earth lies in the darkest part of the shadow (the umbra). The dark part is where all of the Sun's light is blocked by the Moon. During a solar eclipse, the Moon's umbra makes a narrow path as it moves across Earth's surface. The width of this shadow never exceeds 274 km (170 mi). Sometimes only the penumbra reaches Earth. When that happens, part of the Sun is visible during the eclipse.

Of course, Earth can cast a shadow, too. We enter its shadow every evening after sunset. And we emerge from its shadow every morning at sunrise. Sometimes we can see Earth's shadow on the Moon. This is called a lunar eclipse because the Moon becomes partially hidden by Earth's shadow. This can happen when the Sun, Earth, and a full moon all lie along the same line, as shown in Figure 17b. Because Earth's atmosphere bends some sunlight around Earth, our view of the Moon is never totally blocked by Earth's shadow. Even if the Moon enters the dark umbra of Earth's shadow, some sunlight reaches the Moon. The Moon darkens and takes on a copper color, but it doesn't disappear the way the Sun does during a total eclipse.

There are at least two, but never more than five, solar eclipses each year. Lunar eclipses occur just about as often. However, the most eclipses,

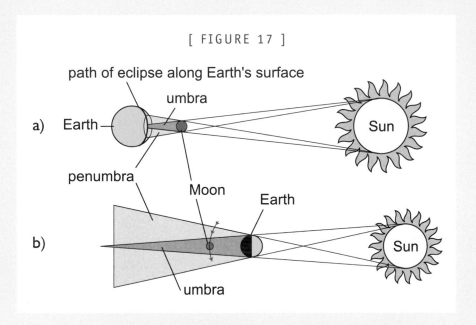

[ FIGURE 17 ]

a) path of eclipse along Earth's surface
umbra
Earth
Sun

penumbra
Moon
Earth

b)
Sun

umbra

17 a) **An eclipse of the Sun (solar eclipse—not to scale) is shown.**
**b) An eclipse of the Moon (lunar eclipse—not to scale) is**
**shown. The Moon is shown passing through Earth's umbra.**

both solar and lunar, that can occur in one year is seven. You might wonder why we don't have solar and lunar eclipses every month, since full and new moons occur monthly. The reason is that the Moon's orbit is not exactly on the same plane as Earth's orbit about the Sun. As a result, the Sun, Moon, and Earth are seldom lined up exactly with one another.

It is always safe to view an eclipse of the Moon because the light from the Moon is quite dim. **But never look at the Sun!** Even during an eclipse, the Sun is so bright it can cause severe damage to your eyes. One way to view a solar eclipse is to look at a pinhole image of the Sun. Make a pinhole in one side of a large cardboard box. Turn the box so the pinhole faces the Sun. With your back to the Sun, place the box over your head. You can view the Sun's image on a sheet of white paper taped to the inside wall of the box opposite the pinhole. Sunlight entering the box through the pinhole forms an image on the white paper. If you use a pegboard, you can see a lot of images of the Sun. You might call them eclipsed Sun dapples.

# 3.2 A Model of a Solar Eclipse

**Materials:**
- frosted lightbulb in socket
- penny or another coin
- scissors
- drinking straw
- file card or paper pad

**Do not do this experiment outdoors with the Sun!**

It's easy to make a model of a solar eclipse. Use an ordinary frosted lightbulb to represent the Sun. A penny or another coin can represent the Moon. Use scissors to make a slit about 0.6 cm (0.25 in) long in one end of a drinking straw, as shown in Figure 18a. The slit in the end of the straw will hold the coin. The straw serves as a handle.

Your head can represent Earth. Your eye can represent a place on Earth where the eclipse can be seen. Stand several feet from the glowing lightbulb. Hold the coin in front of one eye and move it until it blacks out part or all of the lightbulb (see Figure 18b). The coin's shadow falls on your eye and blocks your view of at least part of the bulb. In the same way, the Moon during a solar eclipse casts a shadow on Earth and blocks out at least a part of the Sun.

Move the coin closer to your eye. Does it block out more or less of the bulb as it moves closer to your eye? Slowly move the coin farther from your eye. Does the coin block out more or less of the bulb as you move it away? Hold the coin far enough away so that it blocks the center part of the lightbulb but leaves a ring of light around the edge. This is what happens during what is called an annular eclipse. In an annular eclipse, a thin ring of light is still visible all around the edge of the Sun.

You can also move the coin so that it blocks out the top, bottom, or one side of the lightbulb. This is what happens during a partial eclipse when the Sun and Moon are not quite in line with your location on Earth. As you might guess, you are more likely to see a partial eclipse than a total eclipse.

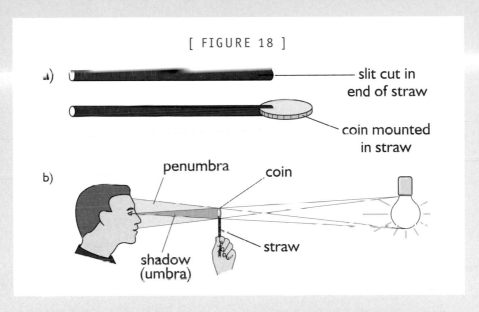

[ FIGURE 18 ]

a) slit cut in end of straw

coin mounted in straw

b) penumbra    coin

shadow (umbra)

straw

18 a) Make a small slit in one end of a drinking straw. Mount a small coin in the straw. b) The coin, which corresponds to the Moon, casts a shadow on your eye. The lightbulb represents the Sun; your eye represents Earth.

Take yourself out of the model by using a file card or a paper pad to represent Earth's surface. Hold the card or pad about 1 m (3 ft) from the glowing lightbulb. Then bring the coin near the lightbulb so you see its dark shadow (umbra) on the paper. Now slowly move the coin (Moon) away from the paper (Earth's surface). You will see the dark umbra grow smaller, while the fuzzy penumbra that surrounds it grows larger. At a certain point, the umbra disappears and only the fuzzy penumbra remains. This corresponds to an annular eclipse. During an annular eclipse, even if you are at the center of the Moon's shadow, you can see a ring of light around the Sun's blacked-out center.

# 3.3 A Model of a Lunar Eclipse

Materials:

- Styrofoam or other soft, opaque spheres; one 5 cm (2 in) in diameter, the other 1.2–1.3 cm (0.5 in) in diameter
- stick 1.5 m (5 ft) long
- 2 small finishing nails
- tape
- sunlight

To make a model of a lunar eclipse, tape a finishing nail to each end of a stick, as shown in Figure 19. Put the balls on the nails as shown. The large ball represents Earth. The smaller ball represents the Moon, which has a diameter that is a bit more than one-quarter of Earth's diameter. Since Earth and the Moon are about 30 Earth diameters apart, the stick is 1.5 m (60 in or 5 ft) long. In that way, the Earth and Moon parts of the model are to scale. [If you prefer, you can cut the scale in half by using a stick 0.75 m (30 in or 2.5 ft) long and spheres that are 2.5 cm (1 in) and 0.6 cm (0.25 in) in diameter, respectively.]

For a Sun, you can use the real Sun. It is very much out of scale for the rest of the model, but the light rays from the Sun are almost parallel anyway. Hold the stick so Earth is closest to the Sun, as shown in Figure 19. Tip and turn the stick until the Sun, Earth and Moon are in line. When they are, Earth's shadow will fall on the Moon. Turn the stick slightly in a horizontal direction. You can see the Moon move into and out of Earth's shadow. If you look closely, you can see that Earth's shadow on the Moon is curved. It was Earth's curved shadow on the Moon that led the astronomers of ancient Greece to believe that Earth was a sphere (a ball).

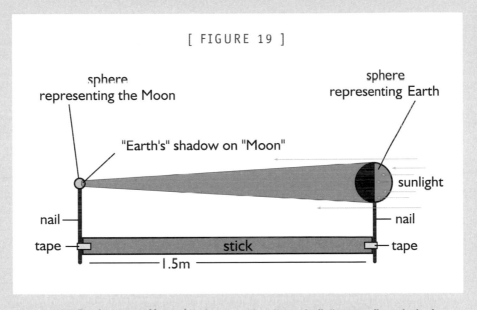

[ FIGURE 19 ]

sphere
representing the Moon

sphere
representing Earth

"Earth's" shadow on "Moon"

sunlight

nail

nail

tape

stick

tape

1.5m

A model of a lunar eclipse is shown. The "Earth," "Moon," and their separation are to scale.

# 🏆 3.4 Sun and Direction

Materials:
- chalk
- magnetic compass

For hikers, canoeists, boaters, and other travelers, the Sun is more than a source of light and energy. It can also indicate direction. The Sun's position or the direction of the shadows it casts can help you find a direction—north, south, east, or west. If you know one direction, you can find the others. After doing this experiment, you will be able to use the Sun to find direction.

To see one way to use the Sun to find direction, watch to see where the Sun rises tomorrow morning or the next clear morning. Also watch to see where it sets tonight or on the next clear evening. **Never look directly at the Sun when it is above the horizon. It can damage your eyes!**

Watch for the sunrise and sunset each month over the course of a year. Choose a point where you can see the rising Sun clearly. Use a piece of chalk to mark the point where you stand to watch the sunrise. If possible, choose the same point to watch both sunrise and sunset. Stand in that same place each time you watch the Sun rise or set. In your science notebook, record the position that you see the Sun on the horizon as it rises. Record the place where you see the Sun set on the horizon. Your record for the first day of this experiment might look like Table 6. If you wish, you might also record the time of sunrise and sunset as well.

## TABLE 6
### Position of the Sun on the Horizon as it Rises and Sets

| Date | Me | Sunrise | Me | Sunset |
|------|-----|---------|-----|--------|
| Sept. 10 | At center of entrance to garage (X marks the spot) | Just left of big pine tree in Mrs. Jones's yard | At center of entrance to garage (X marks the spot) | Behind Mrs. Smith's house |

To make a rough estimate of the Sun's direction at sunset and sunrise, hold a compass at the place or places where you watched the Sun rise and set. Be sure to hold the compass away from metals such as a belt buckle. If it is working properly, the compass needle will point in a northerly direction, but it is not likely to point to true north. That is, it probably will not point toward the North Pole. The North Pole is almost directly beneath the North Star. In what general direction did the Sun rise? In what general direction did the Sun set?

## Science Fair Project Idea

Repeat this experiment on about the twentieth of each month for at least a year. Always stand in the same place to watch each sunrise and each sunset. Does the Sun rise in the same place on the horizon every day? Does the Sun set at the same place on the horizon every day?

# 3.5 Making a Shadow Clock

Materials:

- an adult
- wooden board or sheet of cardboard about 30 cm (12 in) on a side
- finishing nail 5–8 cm (2–3 in) long
- hammer
- scissors
- sheet of paper
- ruler
- tape
- sunny, level place outdoors
- stones (if cardboard is used)
- magnetic compass
- pencil
- watch

From your experiments earlier in the chapter, you know that the Sun appears to move from an easterly to a westerly direction each day. As it moves, the shadows it casts change. They change both in length and direction. Early Egyptians used a stick's changing shadow to make a clock. The direction that we call clockwise (the direction that the hands of a clock move) probably came from the movement of a shadow clock's hand. In fact, the earliest clocks were less accurate than the sundials that were used to set them.

Find a board or a sheet of cardboard about 30 cm (12 in) on a side and a finishing nail 5–8 cm (2–3 in) long. **Ask an adult** to use a hammer to drive the nail a short distance into the board or push it into the cardboard. The nail should be near the middle of one end of the board, about 5 cm (2 in) from the edge (see Figure 20a).

Use scissors to make a 5-cm (2-in) slit at the edge of the center of the long side of a sheet of paper. The slit allows you to slide the paper past the upright nail. Tape the paper to the wood or cardboard and put it in a

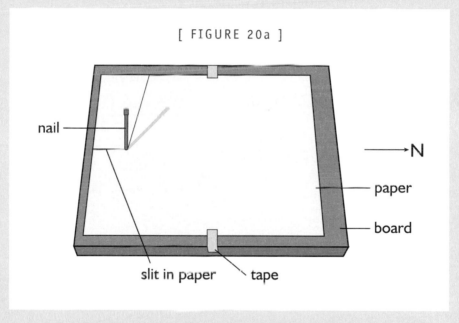

[ FIGURE 20a ]

nail

→N

paper

board

slit in paper     tape

A nail in a board will cast shadows on a sheet of paper. Draw along the nail's shadow at different times.

sunny, level place outdoors, shortly after sunrise. If you use a cardboard base, put stones on its corners to hold it in place. Use a compass to find south. Be sure the nail is on the south side of the paper.

Use a pencil to mark the position of the nail's shadow on the paper at 1-hour intervals throughout the day. Label each line you draw with the time you read on a watch, as shown in Figure 20b.

Mark the position of the board so you can put it in exactly the same place several days, weeks, or months later. Compare the times on the shadow clock with times on your watch during a day several days after you make the shadow clock. Do the same thing a week later. Do it again a month later. Do the times on your shadow clock still agree with the times on your clock or watch after several days? after a week? after a month? Do you think the Egyptian shadow clock was a very accurate timepiece? Do you think the Egyptians cared? How do you think they measured time at night?

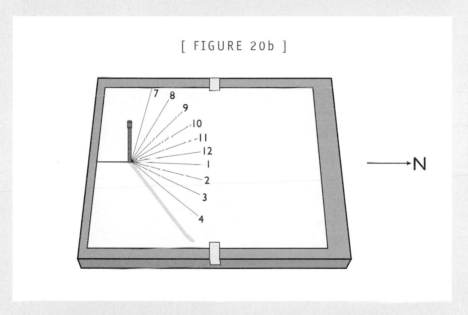

[ FIGURE 20b ]

→N

Label the lines with the times at which you draw them.

## Chapter 4

# The Moon: Our Neighbor in the Sky

**THE MOON IS OUR CLOSEST NATURAL NEIGHBOR IN THE SKY.** It revolves around Earth as our only natural satellite. There are many other much smaller satellites going around (orbiting) Earth, but they were put there by humans.

As you probably already know, the Moon appears to be about the same size as the Sun, but it is really much smaller. It looks as big as the Sun because it is much closer to us than the Sun is. The Sun is approximately 150 million kilometers (93 million miles) from Earth, while the Moon is only about 384 thousand kilometers (239 thousand miles) away. Because the Moon is so close to us, its diameter (width), which is 3,480 km (2,160 mi), appears to be as big as the Sun's diameter. But, in fact, the Sun's diameter (1,400,000 km, or 868,000 mi) is almost 400 times bigger than the Moon's and 109 times bigger than Earth's. In this chapter, you will see how the distance to the Moon can be measured. And in Experiment 4.4, you will measure the Moon's diameter for yourself.

The Moon's distance from Earth changes because its orbit (its path around Earth) is not a perfect circle. Its orbit has an oval shape called an ellipse. When the Moon is closest to Earth, we say it is at *perigee*.

When the Moon is at perigee, it is 356,334 km (221,463 mi) from Earth. When the Moon is farthest from Earth, we say it is at *apogee*. When the Moon is at apogee, it is 405,503 km (251,968 mi) from Earth. Because the Moon's distance from Earth does not change very much, its size seems to be almost constant. However, its shape appears to change quite dramatically.

On Earth's surface, the average temperature is 20°C (68°F). Temperatures above 58°C (136°F) or below -89°C (-129°F) have never been recorded. On the Moon, temperatures change much more. The Moon has no atmosphere and relatively little water to absorb heat. Until recently, it was believed that there was no water on the Moon. However, data from a satellite that orbited the Moon in 1994 indicate there may be a shaded reservoir of ice near the Moon's south pole. Because so little heat is absorbed by the Moon, temperatures in lunar darkness fall to -184°C (-300°F), well below the temperature of dry ice (solid carbon dioxide). (We sometimes use the word *lunar* to describe things that are related to the Moon. It comes from the Latin word for moon, *luna*.) In direct sunlight, the average lunar temperature is 101°C (214°F). Even though the Moon's interior is much cooler than Earth's, experiments show that the Moon, like Earth, is still radiating heat into space.

Earth has more than 80 times more mass (matter) as the Moon. As a result, the force of gravity on the Moon is much less than it is on Earth. Someone who weighs 45 kg (100 lbs) on Earth would weigh only 7 kg (17 lbs) on the Moon. That is why astronauts find it so easy to walk on the Moon. But because the force of the Moon's gravity is so small, it cannot prevent gases from escaping its surface. Lacking gases, the Moon has no atmosphere.

The Moon's average speed around Earth is 3,680 kph or 2,287 mph. It completes one orbit in about 27.3 days. But the time between one full moon and the next is 29.5 days. Why does it take two days longer to go from one full moon to the next than it does for the Moon to make one orbit around Earth?

The reason is that while the Moon makes one orbit around Earth, Earth moves along about one twelfth of its orbit around the Sun. Consequently, the Moon has to travel a little more than one full "circle" before it is again in line with Earth and the Sun (see Figure 21).

[ FIGURE 21 ]

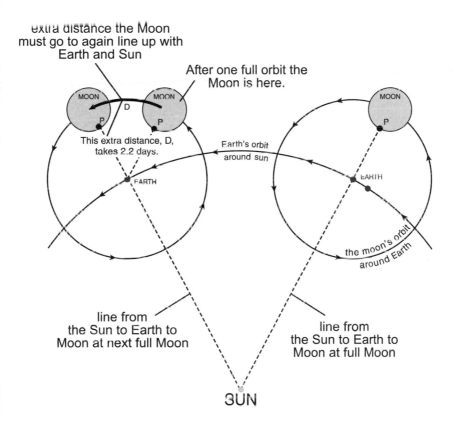

extra distance the Moon must go to again line up with Earth and Sun

After one full orbit the Moon is here.

MOON

MOON

MOON

D

P

P

P

This extra distance, D, takes 2.2 days.

Earth's orbit around sun

EARTH

EARTH

the moon's orbit around Earth

line from the Sun to Earth to Moon at next full Moon

line from the Sun to Earth to Moon at full Moon

SUN

The Moon makes a full orbit around Earth in about 27.3 days. However, since Earth orbits the Sun, the time from one full moon to the next is 29.5 days. The Moon has to travel an extra distance (D) to make a point (P) on the Moon (that directly faces Earth) again line up with Earth and Sun to create a full Moon.

As in Earth's crust, the most abundant element on the Moon is oxygen. Of course, the oxygen does not exist as a gas, because the Moon has no atmosphere. Oxygen on the Moon is chemically joined to many other elements. Silicon, too, is abundant on the Moon; so are calcium, aluminum, and magnesium. Unlike Earth, the Moon contains very little hydrogen. That is because the Moon has little water, which is one-eighth hydrogen by weight.

Earth has a molten (liquid) iron core. The movement of the electric charges in the liquid produces a strong magnetic field. Earth's magnetic field makes it possible for us to use a compass to navigate. The Moon may have an iron-rich core, but it has no magnetic field. The information scientists have gathered about moonquakes shows that the Moon is rigid throughout. The solid Moon has no fluid to carry electric charges. There-fore, it has no magnetic field. (In Experiment 4.1, you can see for yourself that moving charges produce a magnetic field.)

Two-thirds of the Moon's surface is made up of highlands that are rugged like mountains. The highlands reflect a lot of light because they are made up of light-colored rocks that contain calcium and aluminum. The smooth, lower portions of the Moon are covered by darker rocks that contain a lot of magnesium, iron, and titanium. These rocks and dirt reflect less light, so we see those areas as the darker regions of the Moon. When humans first looked at the Moon through telescopes, they thought the dark areas were seas. They called them *maria*, the Latin word for sea, and we still call the dark areas maria today.

Many geologists believe the Moon was originally very hot. About 3.5 billion years ago, it had cooled enough to form a thin, solid crust. At that time it was hit by a number of large meteoroids that broke through the new surface. The magma beneath the crust then welled up, flooding the lowlands with lava.

The back side of the Moon—the side we never see—has no maria. Its entire surface is very light. Scientists believe that the crust on the far side of the Moon had become so thick that the meteoroids could not break through it. As a result, lava did not flood the lowlands on the back side of the Moon.

Actually, we do see a little more than half of the Moon. The Moon wobbles slightly as it revolves around Earth. Over time, its wobbling allows us to see almost three-fifths of its surface.

Both the mountains and the maria of the Moon are covered with depressions, called craters. The craters were made by meteoroids (pieces of matter flying through space). Since the Moon has no atmosphere, any meteoroid headed for the Moon will hit its surface and produce a crater. Most meteoroids that approach Earth burn up as they pass through our oxygen-rich atmosphere. The streak of light that marks a meteoroid's path in the sky is called a meteor. Meteors are often called shooting stars. But they are not stars. They are actually chunks of rock moving through space that happen to enter Earth's atmosphere. They glow with light because they are burning. If any part of a meteoroid reaches Earth's surface, it is considered a meteorite.

Materials:

-an adult

-long piece (several feet) of insulated copper wire

-magnetic compass

-flashlight battery (D-cell)

-wire stripper or knife

-clear plastic tape

It is believed that the Moon does not have a liquid core because scientists have found it has no magnetic field. Because Earth has a liquid core, electric charge can move inside Earth. Moving charges give rise to magnetic fields.

To see that moving charges produce a magnetic field, **ask an adult** to use a wire stripper or a knife to remove about an inch of insulation from each end of a wire. Use pieces of clear plastic tape to hold the middle region of the long wire on top of a compass. The wire should be parallel to the compass needle, as shown in Figure 22. Touch the ends of the wire to opposite ends of a D-cell. When you do this, electric charge can flow through the wire from one end of the battery to the other. What happens to the compass needle when the charges move? What changes if you turn the D-cell around? What changes if you put the wire under instead of on top of the compass?

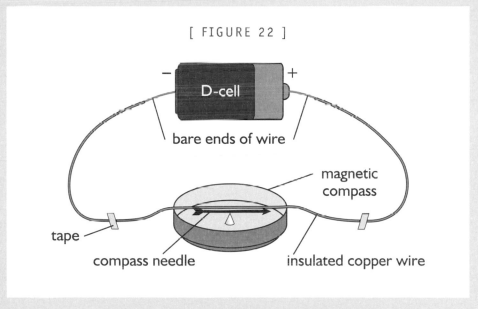

[ FIGURE 22 ]

**Moving charges produce a magnetic field.**

# 🏆 4.2 Moon Observations

Materials:
- daily newspaper with information about the Moon
- Internet access

If you did Experiment 1.4, you have already learned a lot about the Moon by just watching it and its place in the sky. Continue to look for the Moon as often as you can. Each time you see it, note its place in the sky and its distance from the Sun. Record your observations and make drawings of what it looks like.

Daily newspapers have information about the Moon, which is usually printed in the weather section. Use the newspaper to find the date on which a new moon occurs. Several days after the date of a new moon, look for the Moon as the Sun sets.

It is perfectly safe to look at the Moon as much as you want, but **never look directly at the Sun. It can cause permanent damage to your eyes!**

What does the Moon look like as the Sun sets? Draw a picture of it. Where is it in the sky (in what direction)? Which side of the Moon, the side closer to the Sun or the side farther from the Sun, is brighter?

Visit the Web site address <http://aa.usno.navy.mil> to find out more about the Moon. Enter the name of your town or city and you will obtain information about your specific location.

## MEASURING THINGS IN THE SKY

Distances in the sky are usually measured as angles. Sometimes the Sun and Moon appear close together. They might be less than 10° apart because they lie almost on the same imaginary line extending from your eye into space. Actually, they are about 150 million kilometers (93 million miles) apart. The Moon is much closer to Earth than the Sun (see Figure 23). Stars are even farther away than the Sun. When people say a star is close to the Moon, they mean that the angle in the sky between the Moon and the star is small.

[ FIGURE 23 ]

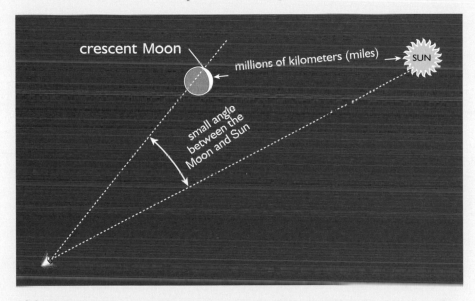

Although the Sun and Moon may appear close together in the sky, they are really millions of kilometers (miles) apart. They appear to be close when the angle we see between them is small.

If you hold your fist toward the sky at arm's length as shown in Figure 24a, it will cover approximately 10° in the sky. To see that each fist really is equal to about 10°, start with one fist closed and extended toward the horizon. Go fist-on-fist upward as shown in Figure 24b, until one arm points straight up. You will find it takes just about nine fists to reach this point. Since from horizontal to straight up is 90°, each fist must cover about 10° (9 × 10°= 90°). How do your results compare with those provided in Experiment 1.4, the newspaper, and the Web site?

## MEASURING THE SEPARATION OF MOON AND SUN AT SUNSET

To find the distance between the Sun and the Moon at sunset, cover the Sun with one hand as you begin (see Figure 25). **Never look directly at the Sun. It can cause permanent damage to your eyes!** Then find how many fists separate the Sun and Moon. Record the number of fists separating them in your science notebook, along with the date and time. Where is the Moon in the sky? That is, in what direction do you have to look to see it? Is it in the west, southwest, northwest, south, east, or some other direction? How many fists is it above the horizon? (The angle of the Moon above the horizon is its altitude in the sky.) What happens to the Moon after the Sun sets? Does it follow the Sun? Does it move east or west in the sky? Check your findings with the information presented in Experiment 1.4, the newspaper, and the Web site.

In your notebook, record the date, time, location of the Moon in the sky, number of fists between the Sun and Moon, the Moon's altitude, direction the Moon moves, and any other information you think might be useful. Your first record might look like the one in Figure 26.

Try to observe the Moon at about the time of sunset each clear evening for the next few days. Make the same measurements you made before and record them in your notebook. What happens to the shape of the Moon during these days? What happens to the distance (number of fists) between the Moon and Sun from one day to the next? What happens to the Moon's

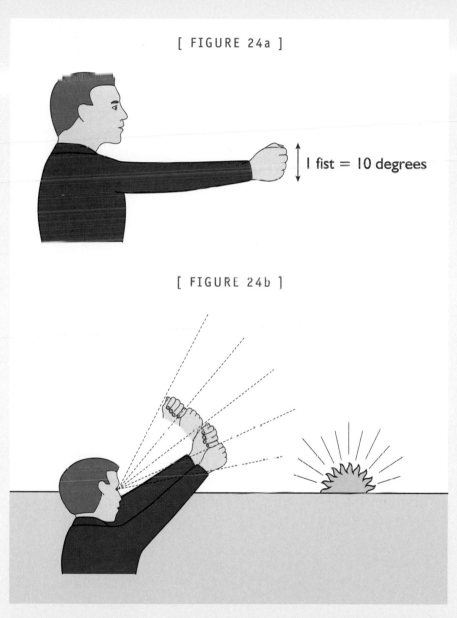

[ FIGURE 24a ]

I fist = 10 degrees

[ FIGURE 24b ]

**24 a) One fist at arm's length covers about 10° in the sky. b) You can see that this is true by going fist-on-fist upward from the horizon. You will find that it takes nine fists to reach an overhead position.**

[ FIGURE 25 ]

SUN

Cover the Sun with one hand as you begin to measure the distance (angle), in fists, between the Sun and Moon.

location in the sky at sunset as the days pass? Is the Moon moving more to the east or to the west of the Sun as days go by? What does this tell you about the time that the Moon rises? Is it rising earlier or later each day?

## FINDING THE MOON BEFORE SUNSET

During the days that you are observing the Moon at sunset, try to find it earlier in the day. Can you see the Moon in the daytime? If you can see it, where is it in the sky? Record any observations in your notebook.

See if you can find the Moon shortly after it rises. Where (in what direction) would you expect to see it rise? At about what time would you expect to see it rise?

## FINDING THE MOON AFTER SUNSET

After you have seen a full moon at sunset, can you see the Moon at sunset on the next night? on the night after that? Can you find the Moon after sunset on these nights? If you can, when does it set? What happens to the Moon's setting time as days pass? What has happened to the Moon's shape?

Approximately how many fists does the Moon move in 1 hour? How could you estimate the distance (angle) between the Sun and Moon even if the Sun has set?

[ FIGURE 26 ]

| DATE | TIME | MOON'S DIRECTION | ANGLE BETWEEN SUN AND MOON | MOON'S ALTITUDE | DIRECTION OF MOON'S MOTION | HOW THE MOON LOOKS |
|------|------|------------------|---------------------------|-----------------|---------------------------|--------------------|
| 12/6 | 4:45 P.M. | SW | 2 Fists | 3 Fists | E to W | |
| | | | | | | |
| | | | | | | |
| | | | | | | |
| | | | | | | |
| | | | | | | |
| | | | | | | |
| | | | | | | |
| | | | | | | |
| | | | | | | |

**This chart shows the beginning of a record to keep track of the Moon over time.**

## FINDING THE MOON IN THE MORNING

After you can no longer see the Moon at sunset, begin looking for it early in the morning, before, during, and after sunrise. What has happened to the Moon's shape? How far is it from the Sun? Is it east or west of the Sun? Which side of the Moon (left or right) is now the brighter side? Is this the side nearer to or farther from the Sun?

As the days pass, does the Moon move closer to or farther from the Sun? What does this tell you about the Moon's rising time? What happens to its shape as the days pass?

 **Science Fair Project Idea**

Continue your observations of the Moon for several months. You will begin to see a pattern to the Moon's motion and changing appearance. How much time passes between one full moon and the next? Look to see where the full moon rises on the horizon.

Materials:

-dark room
-lamp with bright lightbulb
-partner
-light-colored ball, about 5–10 cm (2–4 in) in diameter, mounted on a stick (a Styrofoam ball works well)
-clay

To make this model of the Moon, Earth, and Sun, you need a dark room. Turn on a lamp with a single, bright lightbulb at one end of the room. Have a partner stand beside you holding a Styrofoam ball or another light-colored ball mounted on a stick. If the ball is made of Styrofoam, the stick can be pushed into the ball. If the ball is solid, use some clay to mount it on the stick. Have your partner stand to your left while you face the light, as shown in Figure 27.

In this model, the light represents the Sun. Your head represents Earth. The light-colored ball represents the Moon. Since you are facing the light, the model now represents Earth at noon, when the Sun is in the middle of its path across the sky. The Moon (the ball in this model) is to the east. Slowly turn your head and body toward the east (counterclockwise, toward the Moon). Your turning represents Earth as it rotates on its axis. You see the Moon rise in your model. After making one quarter of a turn, the Sun (lightbulb) will be on your right (west). It is now a setting Sun. The Moon is directly in front of you, so it is in the middle of the sky.

Figure 28a shows Earth (your head), Moon (ball), and Sun (lightbulb) in your model from above. You (Earth) are facing the Moon after one quarter of a turn. Half the Moon you see is bright; the other half is dark. Have you

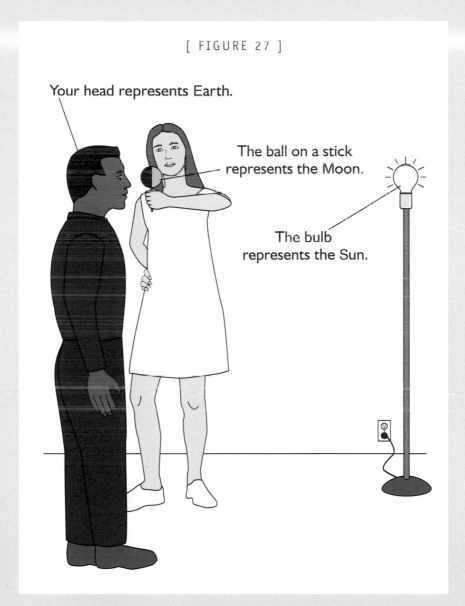

[ FIGURE 27 ]

Your head represents Earth.

The ball on a stick represents the Moon.

The bulb represents the Sun.

A model of Earth, Moon, and Sun shows how the Moon's appearance changes over time.

[ FIGURE 28 ]

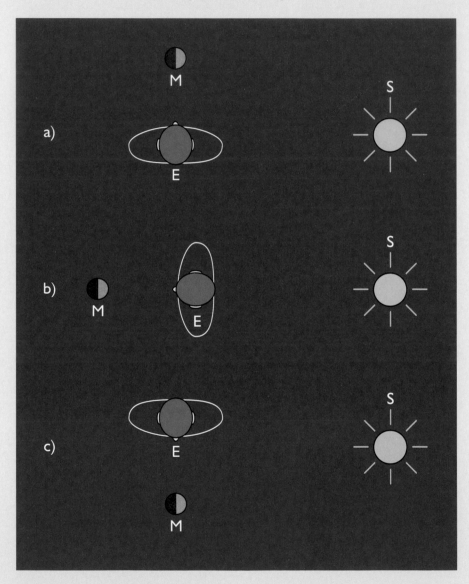

This model of Earth (E), Moon (M), and Sun (S) uses your head for Earth, a lightbulb for the Sun, and a ball for the Moon at a) first quarter; b) full moon; c) third quarter.

ever seen the Moon when it looked like this? If you have, was the Sun setting or near its setting time when the Moon was in the middle of the southern sky?

Now continue to turn slowly to your left to represent the rotating Earth. You will see the Moon set after another quarter turn. As you continue to turn, you will see the Sun rise and move slowly across the sky. Then you will again face the Moon.

In this model, the Moon moves slowly around Earth. After a week (seven full turns of Earth) the Moon will have moved to a point where it is on the opposite side of Earth from the Sun. To represent this model, have your partner slowly move the Moon (ball) one quarter of the way around you while you make seven complete rotations (turns). Your partner should also slowly turn the stick so that the same side of the Moon always faces Earth. Watch what happens to the Moon's appearance as you make these turns. When you face the Moon now, as shown in Figure 28b, it will be a full moon. (If the Moon lies in the shadow of your head, have your partner raise the stick to lift it above your shadow.)

During another seven turns of Earth (your head), the Moon will move slowly to the position shown in Figure 28c. At this point, again only half the Moon you see is bright. But it is now the other half that receives the "sunshine." After another seven turns of Earth, the Moon will lie between Earth and the Sun. Since no reflected light can reach you, you will not see the Moon. It is a new moon. Of course, a room is not a perfect model of space. Some light reflected by the walls and ceiling will reach the ball. This makes the dimly-lighted ball visible. In the space around the real Moon, there are no walls or ceilings to reflect light.

Repeat the experiment once more. While you (Earth) turn about 28 times, have your partner move the Moon once around you. Then give your partner a chance to be Earth while you move the Moon slowly about Earth.

## ABOUT THE MODEL

A good model will agree with what is found in the real world. So let's consider how well the model you tested agrees with what you have seen in the real world. For any one day (one full turn of your head), did the Moon look pretty much the same?

Over the course of a month (one full circle of the ball around you), you saw the Moon's (ball's) appearance change. Did these changes match the way you saw the real Moon change in the sky? That is, did it go from a thin crescent to a half-moon, to a full moon, to another half-moon (with the opposite side bright), to another crescent (but reversed), and then dark (new moon) as it passed between Earth (your head) and the Sun (lightbulb)?

If your answers to these questions are all yes, and they probably are, then the model of the Moon is a good one. The model shows that as Earth rotates on its axis, the Moon moves around Earth about once each month.

Figure 29 is a diagram of the actual model. It shows the Moon orbiting (going around) Earth as Earth orbits the Sun. The actual time between new moons (when the Moon passes between Earth and the Sun) is 29.5 days. Since all the months except February have 30 or 31 days,

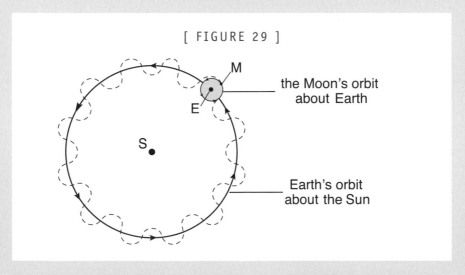

[ FIGURE 29 ]

The actual model is one in which the Moon orbits Earth as Earth orbits the Sun. The path of the Moon as seen from the Sun is shown by the dotted line. (The diagram is not to scale.)

there can be two full moons in one month. When this rare event happens, the second full moon is called a blue moon.

Look at your calendar. Will there be a blue moon this month? this year? What do people mean when they say "once in a blue moon"?

## THE DISTANCE TO THE MOON

One way to measure the distance to the Moon is to aim a radar or laser beam at the Moon. The beam reflects off the Moon and returns to Earth. By measuring the time between the moment the beam is sent and the moment it returns, the distance to the Moon can be calculated. It can be calculated because we know that radar and laser beams both travel at the speed of light, which is 300,000 km/sec (186,000 mi/sec). It takes about 2.6 seconds for the beam to travel to the Moon and back. The total distance the laser light or radar beam travels is 780,000 km (484,000 mi). (This is because 300,000 km/sec times 2.6 sec equals 780,000 km.) But, the beam has traveled to the Moon and back. We must therefore divide by 2, making the distance to the Moon about 390,000 km (242,000 mi).

**Materials:**

- pencil
- ruler
- file card
- scissors
- meterstick or yardstick
- clay

Knowing the distance to the Moon makes it easy to find its size. Use a pencil and a ruler to draw a square 0.6 cm (0.25 in) long and wide near the center of a file card. Cut out the square with scissors. Use a small piece of clay to mount the file card near the end of a meterstick or yardstick, as shown in Figure 30a. Hold one end of the meterstick or yardstick close to one eye. Turn the other end toward the Moon. Start with the card far from your eye so that the Moon fits inside the square. Slowly move the card toward your eye along the stick until the Moon just fits inside the square, as shown in Figure 30b. The length of the square now matches the diameter (width) of the Moon.

As you can see from Figure 30c, the little triangle between your eye and the square in the file card is a part of the big triangle between your eye and the Moon. As a result, the length of the little triangle divided by its base (0.6 cm, or 0.25 in) will equal the distance to the Moon divided by the Moon's diameter. You can find the length of the little triangle divided by its base. It is the distance from the end of the stick (where your eye was) to the file card divided by the length of the square hole (0.6 cm, or 0.25 in). For example, if the card was 72 cm (30 in) from the end where your eye was, then that length divided by 0.6 cm (0.25 in) is:

$$72 \text{ cm} \div 0.6 \text{ cm} = 120,$$
$$\text{or } 30 \text{ in} \div 0.25 \text{ in} = 120$$

As you can see, the result is the same whether you use centimeters or inches. This tells us that the length of the big triangle (390,000 km, or 242,000 mi) divided by its base (the Moon's diameter) is also 120. If the

[ FIGURE 30 ]

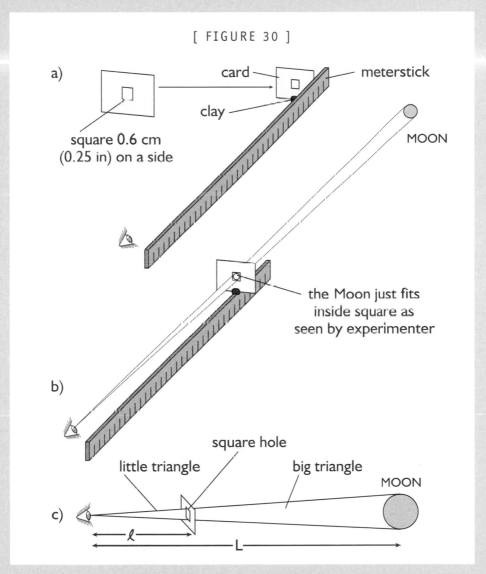

a) card — meterstick

clay

square 0.6 cm
(0.25 in) on a side

MOON

the Moon just fits
inside square as
seen by experimenter

b)

square hole

little triangle

big triangle

MOON

c)

ℓ

L

30 a) Cut a 0.6-cm square in a file card. Mount the card on a meterstick.
b) Move the card until the Moon just fits inside the square hole.
c) The little triangle from your eye to the square is part of the big
triangle from your eye to the Moon. Therefore, $l \div 0.6\text{cm} = L \div$
diameter of the Moon.

distance to the Moon is 120 times its diameter, then dividing its distance by 120 should give us its diameter:

$$390{,}000 \text{ km} \div 120 = 3{,}250 \text{ km,}$$
$$\text{or } 242{,}000 \text{ mi} \div 120 = 2{,}017 \text{ mi}$$

What is the diameter of the Moon according to your measurements?

# 4.5 Using Binoculars to Get a Closer Look

Materials:
- binoculars or telescope

When Galileo turned the telescope he had made toward the Moon in 1610, he opened a new age. Suddenly, his view of the universe changed. And with time, so did the view of all humans. In 1610, all heavenly bodies were believed to be perfectly smooth spheres. But Galileo saw a Moon covered with craters and mountains and the shadows cast by both in sunlight.

You can see what Galileo saw. You can share with him a view that shows that the Moon is far from smooth. You can see a Moon scarred by meteoroids. Most meteoroids that enter Earth's atmosphere burn up. But many meteoroids strike the Moon's surface, because the Moon has no atmosphere.

To see the Moon as Galileo saw it nearly four hundred years ago, you will need binoculars or a telescope. Focus the binoculars on the Moon. You will see a pockmarked surface showing where meteoroids have hit the Moon. If you have a telescope, or if you know someone who does, you may be able to see the Moon's surface even more clearly.

Try to observe the Moon when it is not full. Look at the part of the Moon that is close to the line dividing the light part of the Moon from the dark part. The shadows there are long. Shadows on Earth are long when the Sun is rising or setting. The shadows along the dividing line on the Moon are long for the same reason. If you were standing on that dividing line, you would see the Sun setting or rising on the Moon's horizon.

How do the shadows close to the edge of the dark part of the Moon compare with those near the bright edge of the Moon? Can you explain why? What do the shadows tell you about the Moon's surface?

Continue to look at the Moon with binoculars or a telescope. Look at it during all its phases. Watch it as it waxes (gets bigger) from new crescent to first quarter to full. Then watch it as it wanes (gets smaller) from full to third quarter to old crescent.

During the Moon's early crescent phase, when it is close to the setting Sun, you will see the rest of the Moon dimly lighted. This is sometimes called "the new moon with the old moon in its arms." The dim lighting is caused by earthshine. Earthshine is sunlight reflected from Earth to the Moon. As the lighted portion of the Moon grows bigger and brighter, the dimly lighted portion is less noticeable. This is similar to turning on an outdoor light in the daytime. The light from the bulb is not noticed in bright sunlight.

Look at a full moon through binoculars or a telescope. How do shadows near the center of the Moon compare with those nearer the edges of the Moon?

Watch the Moon's surface closely month after month. You will see that it always looks the same. We see only one side of the Moon. That means that the Moon must rotate (turn) at the same rate that it revolves about (orbits) Earth (see Figure 31). For thousands of years, humans had never seen the far side of the Moon. It wasn't until a spaceship launched by the Soviet Union made a loop around the Moon and took photographs that we knew what the other side of the Moon looks like.

The Moon is the only celestial body about which we have firsthand knowledge. We have such knowledge because during a three-and-a-half-year period between 1969 and 1972, humans walked on the Moon. But we knew a lot about the Moon and its effects on Earth long before we landed on it. Still, sending humans safely to the Moon and back was truly an amazing feat. Much was learned about the Moon by this direct contact and from the 381 kg (840 lbs) of Moon rocks that astronauts brought back to Earth.

## HUMANS ON THE MOON

Before people first walked on the Moon in 1969, a good bit of exploration had already been done. In 1959, instruments onboard the Soviet Union's *Luna 2* showed there was no magnetic field on the Moon. That information was transmitted to Earth before the spacecraft crashed into the lunar surface. During the same year, the Soviet Union's *Luna 3* orbited the Moon and took

[ FIGURE 31 ]

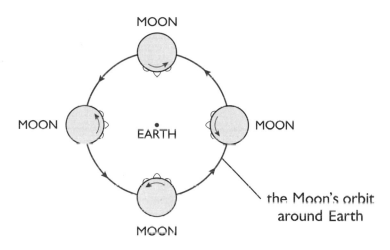

MOON

MOON                    MOON
       EARTH

        MOON

the Moon's orbit
around Earth

**The Moon rotates (turns) at the same rate that it revolves about (orbits) Earth. As a result, we always see the same "face" of the Moon.**

photographs of its back side. That spacecraft was the first to reveal to the world that the back side of the Moon has no maria (dark areas).

In 1965, the United States Ranger probes provided close-up views of the Moon's surface. In 1966, the Soviet spacecraft *Luna 9* made the first successful soft landing on the Moon. That landing made it clear that the Moon was not covered with a thick layer of dust, as some scientists had believed.

From 1966 to 1968, probes that were part of the United States Surveyor program photographed the lunar surface and carried out soil analyses. During the same period, the United States Lunar Orbiter program provided a series of detailed photographs that allowed NASA scientists to draw maps of the Moon's surface.

*Apollo 8* and *Apollo 10* were two missions that carried United States astronauts into orbit around the Moon. The flight of *Apollo 11* then sent

Edwin "Buzz" Aldrin was the second person to walk on the Moon. He and his fellow astronauts—Neil Armstrong and Michael Collins—brought moon rocks back to Earth with them.

a lunar landing module to a soft landing on the surface of the Moon on July 20, 1969. Following the landing, astronaut Neil Armstrong said, "Tranquility Base here. The *Eagle* has landed." A few hours later, Armstrong became the first human to walk on the Moon. As his foot touched the lunar surface, he said, "That's one small step for a man, one giant leap for mankind."

Altogether, *Apollo* spacecraft made six landings on the Moon. In each landing, two people walked on the Moon. A third crew member remained in a command module that stayed in orbit around the Moon until rejoined by the lunar landing module.

The rocks that astronauts brought back to Earth were tested to see how old they were. The age of rocks can be determined by measuring the amount of radioactive uranium and lead in them. Rocks from the lowlands (maria) were found to be about 3.1–3.8 billion years old. The lighter highland rocks were 4–4.6 billion years old. The different ages of the rocks helped to confirm the belief that meteoroids broke through the crust on the near side of the Moon about 3.5 billion years ago. The breaks allowed the molten rock below the surface to well up and flood the lowlands.

Much was learned about the Moon by the astronauts who walked on its surface. In addition to their experiments and the rocks they brought back, they left a number of instruments that continued to relay information to Earth long after the astronauts had left. For example, instruments that record vibrations caused by meteoroids showed that 80 to 150 meteoroids strike the Moon each year. The size of those space rocks varies from 1 to 1,000 kg (2 lbs to 1 ton).

The space shuttle lifts off to carry astronauts into space.

## Chapter 5

# Humans Into Space

**WILL HUMANS EVER RETURN TO THE MOON?** Many people think we should. There are valuable minerals on the Moon that could be mined and used to manufacture the goods on which we all depend. As Earth's minerals become depleted, we may turn to the Moon. In fact, there are plans to build space colonies on orbiting modules near the Moon. These colonies, where some of Earth's excess population could live, would make use of materials extracted from the Moon. So human trips to the Moon may not have ended. Perhaps you will someday walk on the Moon or live in a home that orbits our only natural satellite.

## OUR FUTURE IN OUTER SPACE

Enveloped in flames over the launchpad, the huge vehicle lifts majestically off the ground. Slowly at first, then accelerating, it rises into the sky on a fiery tail. Below, it leaves a long, smoky white trail. Soon it is only a dot. Then it is gone into the heavens.

Another vehicle has been sent into the skies, perhaps to dock with the International Space Station, to repair the Hubble Space Telescope in orbit, to loft artificial satellites, to land on the Moon or on Mars, to look at Venus, Jupiter, or Saturn, or to go out into the universe.

Did early scientists envision such a future in outer space? Sir Isaac Newton (1642-1727), a famous British physicist, mathematician, and astronomer, made our current relationship with outer space possible. He opened the door to our exploration of space when he stated the three laws of motion, mathematically described how gravity works, calculated the speed needed to get an object to go into orbit around Earth, showed what the shape of the orbit would be, and explained why the Moon orbits Earth without falling into it.

Although Isaac Newton lived over 300 years ago, his discoveries are still affecting our daily lives and leading to new knowledge. Recognition of his importance was shown by the Apollo astronauts as they sped through space to the Moon. They sent the following message by radio to Mission Control: "We would like to thank the person who made this trip possible, Sir Isaac Newton."

**Materials:**
- 2 sheets of paper
- book
- plastic drinking cup
- flat piece of metal
- water
- sink

Air exerts a force that opposes the motion of any object moving in it. This opposing force is called air drag or air resistance. As the object barrels through the air, it encounters more impacts from the molecules in front than in back of it, causing it to be slowed.

To see the effect of air drag, crumple a sheet of paper into a tight ball. Drop the ball from shoulder height. Take an identical sheet of paper, uncrumpled, and drop it in the same way. Do they fall at the same speed?

You probably found that the crumpled paper ball drops quickly straight down. The uncrumpled sheet falls much less rapidly than the paper ball because the sheet presents a much larger surface to the moving air molecules than does the crumpled paper ball.

Hold a book horizontally a few feet above a surface. Allow it to drop. Pick it up and place the uncrumpled sheet of paper on top of the book. Hold the book with the paper on it horizontally above the surface as before and allow them both to drop. Does the paper float down or fall quickly?

This time, the paper falls at the same rate as the book. The book protects the paper from the drag of air molecules.

Here is a different experiment. Obtain a plastic drinking cup and a piece of flat metal large enough to cover the mouth of the cup. The back of a metal tray, pan, or cookie sheet could be used. Run several inches of water into a sink. Hold the cup high up over the sink, turn it over, and observe it as it falls mouth down into the sink. Next, fill the cup with water, wet the metal sheet, and place the metal sheet on top of the cup.

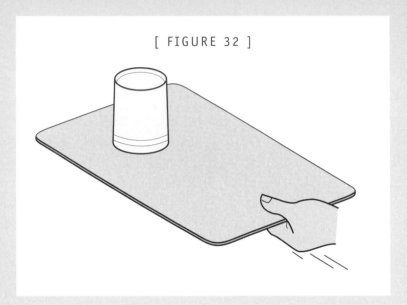

[ FIGURE 32 ]

**A metal sheet with an inverted plastic cup full of water is held over a sink. When the sheet is yanked out from under the cup, the cup and the water fall downward. Does the water spill out while the plastic cup floats down, or do they fall together?**

Hold the metal sheet tightly over the cup while you turn them over together over the sink. Let go of the cup and pull the sheet sharply out from under the cup (see Figure 32), similarly to the way a tablecloth is pulled out from under a set of dishes in that old trick. Does the water drop straight down from the cup while the cup floats down?

Both the cup and the water should drop together into the sink. The water protects the cup from the drag of air molecules. In the absence of air resistance, all objects fall to the ground due to gravity with the same acceleration. Near Earth's surface, objects fall 9.8 m/s faster every second (32 ft/s each second).

**Science Fair Project Ideas**

- Obtain different balls, such as a baseball, Ping-Pong ball, tennis ball, golf ball, and others. Drop them from 4 feet high and then from 10 feet high, measuring the time it takes each to hit the ground. Make a chart of the results. Compare and explain.
- What causes a kite to stay up? What causes it to fall? How fast does it fall? Construct a kite shaped like a parachute. Can you get it to fly? How? Does it stay up by itself? Explain your observations.
- Look up the topic of terminal velocity. Construct several different parachutes to test which design reaches terminal velocity the soonest when dropped. Develop a hypothesis to explain why.

# 5.2 Why Doesn't the Moon Fall

Materials:
- pencil
- drawing paper
- marble
- ruler with groove down the middle
- wok or bowl of similar shape

It is said that Newton developed his law of gravitation while sitting under an apple tree and observing an apple fall. If Newton had really watched the apple fall, he would have known, based on his own laws of motion, that the apple had to have a force acting upon it because it speeded up as it dropped. According to his laws of motion, acceleration occurs only with an unbalanced force. Newton may have conjectured, therefore, that an invisible force was pulling the apple down. How high up could the invisible force be felt? Maybe all the way to the Moon. Maybe throughout the universe. From that observation, perhaps, came the law of universal gravitation.

This law says that all masses attract each other. They do so in proportion to their mass. The attraction decreases rapidly as the distance between the masses widens. Newton stated the law as an exact mathematical equation.

Newton carried out calculations on the orbit of the Moon based on his law of gravitation. His calculations agreed with the known facts about the Moon's orbit. Evidently, it was an invisible force, which Newton called gravity, that was pulling the Moon around Earth.

Newton proposed a thought experiment. It involved firing a cannonball from a cannon. Picture a very high mountain. It is so high up that it is above most of the air in our atmosphere, so that friction cannot interfere. In your imagination, fire a cannonball horizontally out from a cannon at the top of that mountain. What do you predict will be the path of the cannonball?

Did you predict that the cannonball would arc downward? It would move with compound motion outward (first law of motion) and downward (law of universal gravitation). It would keep falling in an arc until it crashed into Earth. That is the most likely scenario.

# Down to Earth?

Now imagine that you load more gunpowder into the cannon and fire the cannonball out faster. What happens this time?

You can expect the cannonball to travel farther before it crashes.

Suppose you keep increasing the charge in the cannon until the ball goes so far out that it misses Earth altogether when it falls.

Draw a picture of this in your science notebook. What will be the path of the falling cannonball as it misses Earth and continues? Remember that Earth is still attracting the ball. Add this to your picture.

See Figure 33 for a diagram similar to one that Newton drew of the trajectory of the cannonball when fired at different speeds. Newton published his diagram of the cannonball's motion in 1687. It showed that when the ball goes fast enough, it keeps falling toward Earth but keeps passing Earth as it falls. Imagine a marble rolling around the inside rim of a plate. The ball would keep going in a straight line if the force from the rim did not drive the ball into a circular motion. A similar process occurs here. The cannonball would fall past Earth and keep going into outer space were it not for Earth's gravitational pull. It is this gravitational attraction that keeps forcing the ball into a circular path. The imaginary cannonball would keep going around Earth forever, a cannonball in orbit.

The same idea explains why the Moon doesn't fall down to Earth. The Moon travels fast enough to keep passing Earth but not fast enough to escape from Earth's gravitational attraction. The Moon is always falling toward Earth and is always missing it.

Newton could never carry out his experiment. He would have needed a mountain 200 miles high, much higher than any on Earth, and he would have needed a cannon with firepower more than four times greater than any cannon that has ever been fired.

You can simulate how the speed with which an object is fired from Newton's imaginary cannon determines whether the object goes into orbit or falls to the ground. Do this by allowing a marble to roll down a grooved ruler held horizontally to the inside of the top edge of a wok or similarly shaped bowl. Adjust the slant of the ruler so that the marble rolls around

[ FIGURE 33 ]

**Newton's cannonball thought experiment.**

the inside of the rim. Then launch the marble at different speeds (slant the ruler both more and then less than the first launch). Observe the path of the marble each time.

When launched too slowly, the ball rolls down into the center of the bowl. When launched fast enough, it circles around the edge of the wok. Friction slows it enough so that gravity eventually pulls it down. It gradually spirals to the bottom of the wok.

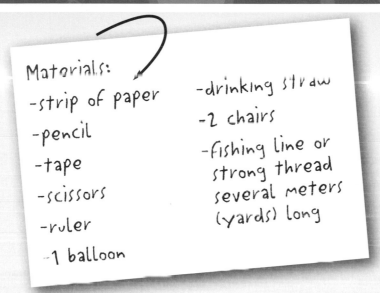

Materials:
- strip of paper
- pencil
- tape
- scissors
- ruler
- 1 balloon
- drinking straw
- 2 chairs
- fishing line or strong thread several meters (yards) long

What causes a rocket to move upward? Newton's third law of motion, the law of action and reaction, makes it possible to send a rocket skyward. Exactly the same law that governs the ascent of a rocket applies to this experiment, in which you will make a balloon "rocket."

To make a nozzle for the balloon rocket, wrap a short strip of paper around a pencil. Tape the end to form a short paper tube and pull the tube off the pencil. Cut the paper tube to about 1.5 cm (about ½ in) long. Slip this tube into the neck of a balloon and tape it firmly in place so that it is 2 to 4 cm (at least 1 in) below the opening. Blow up the balloon and knot or tie it so that the tube is inside the closed neck.

Attach a drinking straw to the outside of the inflated balloon with strips of tape, as shown in Figure 34.

Set up two chairs 2 to 3 meters (2 to 3 yards) apart. Cut a piece of fishing line or strong thread long enough to stretch well past the two chairs. Thread the line through the straw. Tie the line from one chair just below the seat to the other chair at the same height so that the line is tightly stretched.

Pull the balloon along the fishing line so that its neck is at one chair. What, if anything, happens to it? Cut off the knotted end of the

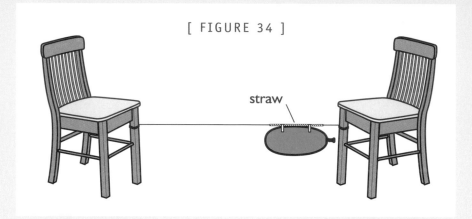

[ FIGURE 34 ]

straw

**A balloon filled with air illustrates Newton's third law of motion. When air jets out of the balloon in one direction, the balloon travels in the opposite direction.**

balloon just above the nozzle. What happens this time? How does Newton's third law explain what you see? What is acting and what is reacting?

When you push the balloon over to one chair, it stays there. When the knot is cut, the balloon shoots along the line toward the other chair. It may look to you as if the air coming out is pushing in one direction so that the balloon simply moves in the other direction. This is not quite why the balloon obeys Newton's third law. Inside the balloon, air molecules are in constant motion, bouncing all over and banging all around inside the skin. There is only one portion of the skin against which they cannot push. That place is where molecules can exit through the neck of the balloon. As a result, the push of the air molecules all around the inside of the balloon is balanced except for the spot where the air exits. Opposite that opening, the unbalanced force of the air molecules pushes the balloon forward, as illustrated in Figure 35.

A rocket is similarly launched into space by violently heated gases that surge against the rocket chamber and out through the opening in the tail. The thrust of the gases in the chamber is unbalanced due to the gases exiting through the opening. The unbalanced force causes the rocket to soar upward. The proof that the propellant force is not due to the gases pushing against the outside air is that a rocket works in airless space.

Once an artificial satellite is in orbit, no fuel is needed to keep it going. It obeys Newton's first law and keeps coasting ahead while falling around Earth in the same way that the Moon does.

What happens to a rocket that is launched to reach a speed greater than the 28,000 km/hr (17,500 mph) needed to get into circular orbit? The faster the rocket goes, the higher its orbit. As the rocket goes higher in orbit, Earth's pull on it decreases. This is because the gravitational attraction between any two objects decreases the farther apart they are.

[ FIGURE 35 ]

unbalanced force
of air molecule impacts

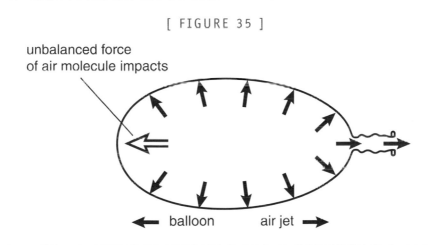

← balloon          air jet →

**This figure shows what happens when the nozzle of an inflated balloon is opened. Before the nozzle was opened, air molecules inside the balloon were beating equally on all sides of the balloon, as indicated by the arrows. The forces exerted on the walls of the balloon by all the air molecules were balanced. When the nozzle of the balloon is opened, air jets out the opening. As a result, the force of the air molecules is no longer balanced. The unbalanced force pushes the balloon in the direction opposite to the exiting air jet.**

If the rocket can be launched with enough velocity, Earth will be unable to pull it into orbit. When that happens, the rocket completely escapes from Earth and travels to outer space. The escape velocity of a rocket from Earth's surface is 40,250 km/hr (25,000 mph), ignoring air friction (see Figure 36).

When a spacecraft or artificial satellite orbits Earth, it encounters scattered molecules of gas that gradually slow it down. As the spacecraft slows down, its orbit becomes lower and lower until it encounters enough atmosphere to send it plunging to Earth.

A spacecraft returning to land on Earth must first be carefully slowed down by firing its rockets. As the craft slows down, its orbit becomes lower until it zings through Earth's atmosphere. Friction, acting as an atmospheric brake, slows the craft until it can be landed safely. Tremendous heat can be produced during reentry into the atmosphere, so special tiles protect the nose of the craft from burning up. To help reduce friction to a safe level, the vehicle enters the atmosphere at a small angle to it.

On March 23, 2001, the 15-year-old failing Russian space station, *Mir*, was deliberately brought down from space in such a way as to be safely destroyed during the reentry process. *Mir* was deorbited with the aid of braking thrusters until it was on a planned path through the atmosphere. Most of it burned up as it zinged back down. The fiery remains of the craft, as planned, plunged into a remote area of the South Pacific Ocean.

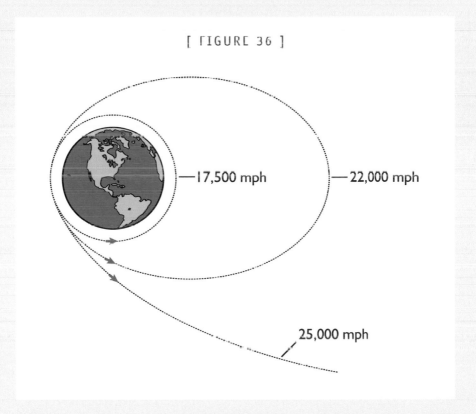

[ FIGURE 36 ]

—17,500 mph —22,000 mph

25,000 mph

**Path of a rocket after launching from Earth at different speeds. At the escape velocity, 25,000 miles per hour, the rocket will shoot off into outer space.**

**Science Fair Project Ideas**

- How does the size of the tail opening affect the speed of a rocket? What is your hypothesis? Repeat the experiment with the rocket balloon of Experiment 5.3 but make changes in the size of the tube in the neck of the balloon. Chart your results and explain them.
- What do you predict would happen if a bigger balloon were used for Experiment 5.3? Find out. Explain your results.
- Does the shape of the balloon make a difference in Experiment 5.3? To find out, use two balloons with different shapes but with the same volume. Explain your results.
- How is the thrust of a real rocket engine controlled by the shape of the gas expansion chamber?
- Can the distance traveled by the rocket balloon of Experiment 5.3 be increased by streamlining? Find out by making a nose cone for the balloon.
- Can you launch a rocket balloon vertically upward on a string? Try tying a string from the ground up a flagpole to use for the upward track for the balloon. How far can you get the balloon to go? What modifications can you introduce to get the balloon to go higher? How well do they work? Suppose you hang on the balloon a small paper cup with a paper clip in it. Can you still get the balloon to rise up the string? How many paper clips can the balloon support before it can no longer rise? Note that at that point the balloon is like a rocket that is too heavy for its engine to lift off the ground.
- Carry out three launchings of a balloon on a string, one horizontally as in Experiment 5.3, one vertically, and one at an angle. Compare the results and explain them.
- Simple rockets can be made from paper tubes. Form a tube by rolling a paper strip around a pencil and taping the end

in place, then freeing the pencil. Tape the upper end of the tube shut. Attach fins to the lower end of the tube so it will not wobble in flight and fall. Experiment to find the best shapes, locations, and numbers of fins. To launch the rocket, blow through a straw into the bottom end or use a more powerful source of propelled air. How does your paper rocket illustrate Newton's third law? List the variables that you altered during this experiment and explain the outcomes. What was the farthest your rocket went? What design made this possible? Why was it effective? **In all rocket tests, be sure that no person or object is close enough to be harmed by the launch or the rocket.**

- Design, construct, and test a more effective rocket than the balloon rocket of Experiment 5.3. Small rockets may be launched using gases produced from a chemical reaction. A safe reaction that produces carbon dioxide as a propellant is a mixture of vinegar and baking soda. Measure how high a carbon dioxide rocket goes. Describe additional improvements and the results of testing. **Do rocket experiments with adult supervision.**

- Build models of actual rockets that have been launched into space using easily available scrap materials such as cardboard tubes, spools, and Styrofoam. Prepare an information sheet for each rocket that you construct, describing the original designer of the rocket, the time period when the rocket was designed, and the rocket's special characteristics.

- What is a two-stage rocket? What is the purpose of the stages? Draw a diagram of a rocket with two or more stages. How much more effective is it than a rocket without stages?

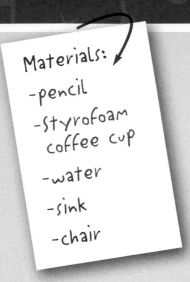

Materials:
- pencil
- Styrofoam coffee cup
- water
- sink
- chair

Once astronauts are in orbit, they float inside the orbiter along with everything else that is not fastened down. There is no up or down inside. In order to direct their motion during a task outside the spacecraft, an astronaut has to use small thrusters on a space pack.

Actually, astronauts at 200 miles up are still well within Earth's gravitational field and are not completely weightless. The gravitational force at that height is about 90 percent of what it is on Earth. Instead, the astronauts are falling all the time, in the same way that the Moon falls around Earth. However, all the objects in the space vessel, and the vessel itself, are falling together, so they all seem to float together.

To show a similar effect, use a pencil to punch a hole near the bottom of a Styrofoam cup. Cover the hole with a finger while filling the cup with water. Holding the cup over a sink, remove your finger from the cup. What happens?

Again cover the hole with your finger and refill the cup. Carry out the rest of this experiment outdoors. Throw the cup straight up and observe. If you have trouble getting it to go straight up, stand on a chair and drop it straight down.

When you hold the cup over the sink and remove your finger, water flows freely through the hole. When you throw the cup straight up, the water stops coming out on the way up and as it falls. This is because both the cup and the water are rising or falling with the same acceleration due to your throw and then to gravity. Compared to each other, the cup and the water are weightless. If a cup of water (no hole in it) were sitting on a scale and you tossed the scale upward with the cup on it, they would similarly fall together so that the scale would read zero. They would be in free fall.

You experience free fall on a swing when it reaches the top of the arc and is about to change direction. At that moment, you and the seat of the swing are weightless. You can get a similar feeling at the top of a roller coaster as it first starts to descend.

Weightlessness in space is called *microgravity*. Astronauts undergo a variety of changes while in a microgravity environment. When gravity no longer acts to pull body fluids downward, body fluids shift from the lower to upper parts of the body. Extended stays may cause a loss of muscle tone, a decrease in production of red blood cells, and an increase in production of white blood cells. Fortunately, most of those effects reverse upon returning to Earth. The astronauts do exercises and ingest a diet designed to minimize those effects.

# Science Fair Project Ideas

- Construct a simulated space capsule. Place within it labeled mock-ups of all the instruments needed to successfully operate the craft. Show the calibration and units for each. Where is each one best located? Why? What facilities are needed for the astronauts to conduct the activities needed for daily living? How are the facilities constructed and where are they placed? How do the astronauts operate the thrusters and the door to the spacecraft? What kind of help does an astronaut need to get into a spacesuit while inside the capsule? What tools must be supplied for everyday activities and for emergencies? You may wish to do this project with partners or with your class at school.

- Construct a device to record the reading on a scale of an object in free fall. One suggestion is to use a small postal scale anchored to a small board. A weight can be sealed onto the platform of the scale. The board can be suspended high up on a rope wound around a pulley. A large piece of foam may be placed underneath to cushion the landing of the board. When the rope is released, the board will fall straight down. A video camera or other photographic device may be placed to record the reading on the postal scale as it descends. Explain the reading.

# 5.5 Finding Your Weight in Space

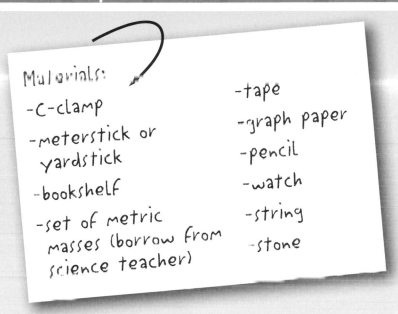

Materials:
- C-clamp
- meterstick or yardstick
- bookshelf
- set of metric masses (borrow from science teacher)
- tape
- graph paper
- pencil
- watch
- string
- stone

During their time in space, astronauts keep records of what they eat, how they feel, their height and weight, and other statistics. But how can they determine their weights in a weightless environment?

Actually, they do not measure their weight; they measure their mass, which is the same everywhere. Since they are weightless, they do not stretch the springs of any scales used to measure weight. Even the equal arm balances used to measure mass in laboratories cannot be used in space. Such balances depend on the equal gravitational pull on the masses at both ends of the balance. However, inertial balances can be used to measure mass anywhere. Such balances do not depend on gravity for their operation.

The inertial balances used in space stations or space laboratories are large enough for a person to sit in. But you can make and calibrate a small model inertial balance quite easily. Use a C-clamp to fasten a meterstick to the side of a bookshelf as shown in Figure 37a. Fasten a 20-g mass to the end of the yardstick with tape. Then measure the time it takes the meterstick to swing back and forth (oscillate) 50 times. Repeat the process again using heavier masses. Each time, record the mass and the time

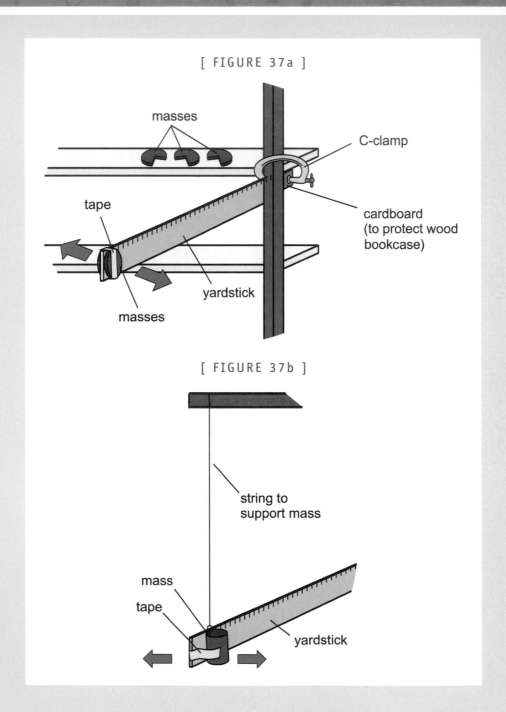

[ FIGURE 37a ]

masses

C-clamp

tape

cardboard
(to protect wood
bookcase)

yardstick

masses

[ FIGURE 37b ]

string to
support mass

mass

tape

yardstick

required for the meterstick to make 50 oscillations. Does the oscillation time of the meterstick depend on the mass attached to the end of the stick?

Plot a graph of the time to make 50 swings versus the mass attached to the meterstick. Plot time on the vertical axis and mass on the horizontal axis. Connect the points you plotted with a smooth line.

Now attach an object of unknown mass to the end of the meterstick. You might use another C-clamp or a stone. Measure the time it takes for the unknown mass to make 50 oscillations. Then use the graph you have made to estimate its mass. If you have a regular balance, you can check the mass of the unknown and see how close your prediction was.

To see that gravity does not enter into this measurement of mass, hang one of the masses you used from a long string so that it does not rest on the meterstick as shown in Figure 37b. Tape it to the meterstick so it will move when the meterstick moves. The mass will now move with the meterstick balance, but it is not exerting any gravitational force on the meterstick. How does the time required to make a certain number of swings now compare with the time it took to make the same number of swings when the mass was pulling downward on the meterstick?

# Answers for Chapter 3

1) 4
2) 4 sq cm
3) 24 sq cm
4) It is 4 times larger (24 sq cm vs. 6 sq cm).
5) 8 times
6) 8 cu cm
7) They are the same.

# FURTHER READING

**Books**

Bochinski, Julianne Blair. *The Complete Workbook for Science Fair Projects.* Hoboken, N.J.: John Wiley and Sons, Inc., 2005.

Carson, Mary Kay. *Exploring the Solar System: A History With 22 Activities.* Chicago: Chicago Review Press, 2006.

McCutcheon, Marc. *The Space Book: Activities for Experiencing the Universe and the Night Sky.* New York: John Wiley & Sons, Inc., 2002.

Moorman, Thomas. *How to Make Your Science Project Scientific.* Revised Edition. New York: John Wiley & Sons, Inc., 2002.

Nicolson, Cynthia Pratt and Paulette Bourgeois. *The Jumbo Book of Space.* Toronto: Kids Can Press, 2007.

Phelan, Glen. *An Invisible Force: The Quest to Define the Laws of Motion.* Washington, D.C.: National Geographic, 2006.

Stott, Carol. *Eyewitness: Space Exploration.* New York: DK Publishing, 2004.

# INTERNET ADDRESSES

**The Museum of Science, Art, and Human Perception.** *Exploratorium.* 2008.
<http://www.exploratorium.edu/index.html>.

**NASA.** *NASA Kids' Club.* 2008.
<http://www.nasa.gov/audience/forstudents/index.html>.

**Society for Science and the Public.** *Science News for Kids.* 2008.
<http://www.sciencenewsforkids.org>.

# INDEX

# ABOUT THE AUTHORS

**Robert Gardner** is an award-winning author of science books for young people. He is a retired high school teacher of physics, chemistry, and physical science.

**Madeline Goodstein, PhD**, is a retired professor of chemistry from Central Connecticut State University. She is the author of numerous science project books with Enslow Publishers, Inc.